PROJECT SUCCESS AND QUALITY

Projects are inherently risky, since they involve some level of uncertainty, doing something new in the target environment, but the percentage of projects seen as a success is still disappointingly low, especially for IT projects. The 'Iron Triangle' of time/cost/quality suggests that all three aspects are equal, but with quantitative methods for monitoring project performance, the focus is primarily on managing cost and time.

This book seeks to redress the balance, explaining the rationale and benefits of focusing more on quality (fitness for purpose and conformance to requirements) before detailing a range of tools and techniques to support rebalancing the management of projects, programmes and portfolios.

It shows how managing project quality actively can reduce costs through minimising wastage, and reduce delays through avoiding rework, leading to improved project success rates and customer satisfaction.

Andrew Wright is a Fellow of the Association for Project Management, a Registered Project Professional, a member of the Institute of Directors and a Visiting Lecturer at the University of Manchester, UK, the University of Cumbria, UK, and University College London, UK.

Therese Lawlor-Wright is a Fellow of the Institute of Mechanical Engineers, a Chartered Mechanical Engineer, a member of the Association for Project Management, a Principal Lecturer in Project Management at the University of Cumbria, UK, and a Visiting Lecturer at the University of Manchester, UK.

PROJECT SUCCESS AND QUALITY

Balancing the Iron Triangle

Andrew Wright and Therese Lawlor-Wright

LONDON AND NEW YORK

First published 2019
by Routledge
2 Park Square, Milton Park, Abingdon, Oxon OX14 4RN

and by Routledge
711 Third Avenue, New York, NY 10017

Routledge is an imprint of the Taylor & Francis Group, an informa business

© 2019 Andrew Wright and Therese Lawlor-Wright

The right of Andrew Wright and Therese Lawlor-Wright to be identified as authors of this work has been asserted by them in accordance with sections 77 and 78 of the Copyright, Designs and Patents Act 1988.

All rights reserved. No part of this book may be reprinted or reproduced or utilised in any form or by any electronic, mechanical, or other means, now known or hereafter invented, including photocopying and recording, or in any information storage or retrieval system, without permission in writing from the publishers.

Trademark notice: Product or corporate names may be trademarks or registered trademarks, and are used only for identification and explanation without intent to infringe.

British Library Cataloguing-in-Publication Data
A catalogue record for this book is available from the British Library

Library of Congress Cataloging-in-Publication Data
A catalog record has been requested for this book

ISBN: 978-0-8153-8038-2 (hbk)
ISBN: 978-0-8153-8039-9 (pbk)
ISBN: 978-1-351-21327-1 (ebk)

Typeset in Bembo
by Servis Filmsetting Ltd, Stockport, Cheshire

For those who struggle everywhere to explain why a focus on quality is not an overhead in a project, but an intrinsic element of all the work, and vital for project success

CONTENTS

List of figures	x
List of tables	xii
Preface	xiv
Acknowledgements	xvi
List of abbreviations	xvii

1. What is quality, and why do priorities need balancing?	1
1.1 What does 'quality' mean?	3
1.2 Definitions of quality	4
1.3 Quality as 'meeting requirements'	5
1.4 A brief history of quality management	7
1.5 Quality management in the project context	11
1.6 Measuring quality	12
1.7 Conclusions of chapter	15
1.8 Bibliography	15

2. Why manage quality?	17
2.1 What are the benefits of effective quality management?	18
2.2 Creating business justification for rebalancing focus on quality	26
2.3 Conclusions of chapter	30
2.4 Bibliography	31

3. Who is responsible for quality?	32
3.1 Everyone is responsible for quality	32
3.2 Quality culture forms the foundation	33
3.3 Quality responsibilities within organisations	36

viii Contents

3.4 *Quality-related roles within projects*   39
3.5 *External services and delegated inspection authorities*   44
3.6 *Conclusions of chapter*   46
3.7 *Bibliography*   46

4. When does quality need to be managed?   48

4.1 *The evolving scope of quality management*   49
4.2 *The toolkit supporting successful delivery during project initiation*   53
4.3 *Tools used to deliver quality during project execution*   58
4.4 *Conclusions of chapter*   60
4.5 *Bibliography*   61

5. Quality management throughout the project lifecycle   62

5.1 *Concept stage*   63
5.2 *Definition stage – getting the customer focus*   63
5.3 *Delivery Stage – turning ideas into reality*   64
5.4 *Hand-over/take-over/go-live stage*   76
5.5 *Benefits realisation stage: warranty, operations and maintenance*   77
5.6 *Conclusions of chapter*   78
5.7 *Bibliography*   79

6. Where does quality need managing?   80

6.1 *In the office*   80
6.2 *The factory production environment – creating quality products*   85
6.3 *On site*   87
6.4 *Conclusions of chapter*   90
6.5 *Bibliography*   91

7. Extending quality management through the supply chain   92

7.1 *Introduction to supply chain quality*   92
7.2 *Synergies between supplier quality assurance and procurement processes*   94
7.3 *Use of supplier auditing in quality assurance*   96
7.4 *The need for clear requirements documentation*   96
7.5 *The need for clear acceptance criteria*   97
7.6 *Quality needs the right relationship with the suppliers*   101
7.7 *Supplier development improves quality management*   101
7.8 *Quality incentives*   102
7.9 *Conclusions of chapter*   104
7.10 *Bibliography*   106

8. Quality analysis techniques   107

8.1 *Measurement and analysis: accuracy and precision*   108
8.2 *Quality management techniques*   110

Contents **ix**

8.3 Conclusions of chapter — 119
8.4 Bibliography — 119

9. Project management techniques vital to quality — 121
9.1 Requirements management — 122
9.2 Change control — 125
9.3 Risk management in project quality — 127
9.4 Measuring project performance in delivering quality — 135
9.5 Capturing, managing and sharing knowledge — 138
9.6 Conclusions of chapter — 143
9.7 Bibliography — 143

10. IT project quality management — 144
10.1 Requirements: the challenge of understanding the goal — 145
10.2 User interface design: including the user in the system — 150
10.3 Training to use IT solutions: people matter — 152
10.4 Performance and other non-functional requirements often missed — 154
10.5 Safety-critical and Control Systems requirements — 155
10.6 Testing and accepting IT solutions — 155
10.7 Conclusions of chapter — 159
10.8 Bibliography — 160

11. The role of published standards in achieving project quality — 161
11.1 Standards supporting quality management — 162
11.2 Project management maturity and performance improvement — 166
11.3 Benefitting from standard operating procedures (SOPs) — 168
11.4 Conclusion: standards support delivering quality, but can't ensure it — 169
11.5 Bibliography — 169

12. Project success and balancing the Iron Triangle — 171
12.1 The iron triangle as an analytical tool — 171
12.2 Conclusion: a culture of quality is needed to balance the iron triangle appropriately — 176
12.3 Bibliography — 177

Glossary of quality terms — 178
Appendix case study: getting the balance right – Rion-Antirion Bridge — 182
Index — 189

FIGURES

1.1 The iron triangle of project management	1
1.2 Convergence of billing systems and consequent operating cost savings	10
1.3 The trade-off between the cost of achieving quality and the cost of failing to	14
1.4 The trade-off between the cost of achieving quality and the cost of failing to in projects	15
2.1 Rion-Antirion Bridge	18
2.2 Trade-off between quality planning and project delay reduction	22
2.3 Schematic financial breakdown of improved quality within the project	29
2.4 Contrasting the initial purchase price with total cost of ownership	30
3.1 The scope of project teamworking	34
3.2 The main steps in introducing a corporate culture change	37
4.1 Advancing scope of quality thinking	49
4.2 How investment in quality reduces cost	52
4.3 'V Model' schematic view of the typical project lifecycle	53
4.4 Quality flow diagram for the project lifecycle	54
5.1 Relationship between quality tools and life-cycle stages	63
5.2 Faulty redesign at Hyatt Regency	72
6.1 Three Mile Island schematic	89
7.1 Return on supplier development	102
8.1 Difference between accuracy and precision	108
8.2 The normal distribution	109
8.3 Varying precision/standard deviation	109
8.4 Basic 5Ys example	112
8.5 Topology of a real 5Ys analysis	112
8.6 The Deming Cycle of continuous improvement	116
9.1 Typical change management process	127

Figures **xi**

9.2 Risk management process	130
9.3 Efficiency versus effectiveness in the project context	135
9.4 Project KPI detecting under-delivery	138
9.5 Distilling insight from data	142
10.1 The 'V model' of system development	146
10.2 Progress comparison of Agile and Waterfall approaches	148
11.1 The BS kitemark	166
11.2 The CE mark	166
12.1 The iron triangle, split into zones for quality management impact assessment	172
12.2 The Iron Pyramid – how quality underpins project success	177
13.1 Rion-Antirion Bridge	183
13.2 Seabed was prepared for pylon base	184
13.3 The pylon bases were constructed in dry dock	185
13.4 The partially completed bases were floated out for further construction	185
13.5 Once the pylon was completed, deck sections were cantilevered out	186
13.6 Dampers now in place	187

TABLES

1.1 Quality in choice of airlines	6
1.2 Quality in choice of bags	6
1.3 Quality in choice of cars	7
2.1 Project issues and risks from cost-cutting	27
3.1 Roles and responsibilities in project quality management (based on PRINCE2)	40
3.2 Additional quality-related roles and responsibilities in large projects	41
3.3 Additional quality roles and responsibilities in project supply chains	42
3.4 Group working versus team working (adapted from Nicholson 1982)	44
5.1 Quality outputs and tools of project definition	64
5.2 Quality outputs and tools of requirements capture	65
5.3 Quality outputs and tools of planning	67
5.4 Quality outputs and tools of contracting	68
5.5 Quality outputs and tools of design	69
5.6 Quality outputs and tools of build	71
5.7 Quality outputs and tools of acceptance	74
5.8 Quality outputs and tools of integration and commissioning	75
5.9 Quality outputs and tools of take-over	77
6.1 Tasking for quality – communications channels	84
7.1 Example service level agreement (SLA)	99
8.1 The seven quality tools	110
8.2 The seven lean wastes	117
9.1 A basic risk log template	134
9.2 Challenges to measuring project performance	137

10.1	Safety-critical and control systems special requirements	156
10.2	Breakdown of IT test types	158
12.1	Quality management assessment of zones in the iron triangle	173
12.2	Glossary of quality terms	180

PREFACE

This book was inspired by personal experiences working in the IT solutions industry (where project failure rate is especially high), and by the Quality Improvement for the Individual programme we participated in when first entering industry at International Computers Limited (ICL).

Its primary aim is to dispel the myth that project quality management is some dull 'policing' activity carried out by specialists who want to slow the project down and overload everyone with tedious bureaucracy, and make it clear that quality is a key foundation of project success that everyone is responsible for. It is a mind-set and a way of working that should be as natural as breathing.

Andrew's vacation jobs as a student were in quality control, for British Oil and Cake Mills and Birds Eye Foods, so the value of quality was driven home right from the start of his career. Therese's vacation work experience included insights into safety at work, in a factory that was putting improved measures in place following a serious accident on a production line.

Andrew started his career in software research, developing artificial intelligence applications, where understanding the requirements was more challenging than delivering the solution. Developing his project management expertise in the manufacturing, defence systems, finance and telecoms sectors, his insights into why projects fail contributed to this book. Becoming a visiting lecturer at the University of Manchester in 2012, he has since taught project management on a range of programmes. He became a Fellow of the Association for Project Management (APM) in 2012 and a Registered Project Professional in 2015. He is actively involved in the APM's Specific Interest Group on Systems Thinking, as this discipline provides a powerful set of tools and techniques to support understanding requirements comprehensively.

Therese's early career involved research into 'Design for Manufacture', at the University of Manchester Institute of Science and Technology (UMIST), ICL and the University of Salford, becoming a Chartered Engineer. She shifted focus when moving to the University of Manchester, to teach and research in the field of project management, developing a strong interest in distance learning and elearning, and becoming a Fellow of the Higher Education Academy. She is a passionate advocate of aligning academic and professional education. She leads the Project Management Group at the University of Cumbria and is a member of the APM and a Fellow of the Institute of Mechanical Engineers.

This book is for project sponsors as well as portfolio, programme and project managers and explores the need to rebalance the focus of project management in favour of quality, for projects to be more successful, more often. It covers the theory and practical understanding of quality management aims, objectives, disciplines, techniques and above all benefits, within the project environment, and describes how those reduce delays and cost escalation.

Throughout this book, we have drawn heavily for inspiration on some key sources:

1. The Association for Project Management Body of Knowledge – this is the distilled wisdom on project management from the UK's leading body of professional project managers.
2. 'Managing Successful Projects with PRINCE2®' – a UK Government-originated publication about using one of the world's leading project management methodologies. The material in this book was developed before the 2017 Edition was published – in the latest PRINCE2 edition, there is much convergence with this book.
3. BS EN ISO 9000:2015 Quality management systems – Fundamentals and vocabulary (BSI, 2015).
4. BS EN ISO 9001:2015 Quality management systems. Requirements – relevant Quality standard (BSI, 2015a).
5. BS EN ISO 9004:2009 Managing for the sustained success of an organization – A quality management approach.
6. BS ISO 10006:2003 Quality management systems — Guidelines for quality management in projects.

We use the term 'product' to refer to anything produced by the project, from documents to bridges, from processes to standards.

Andrew Wright, Therese Lawlor-Wright

11 June 2018

ACKNOWLEDGEMENTS

Thanks to Dr Alan Slater, of Pathfinder Associates Ltd, for his contributions to developing the original course that inspired this book.

Thanks, also, to Professor Andy Gale for facilitating the development of the course behind this material.

We also appreciate the comments and discussions with course delegates and students at the University of Manchester and the University of Cumbria which helped us communicate our ideas.

Finally, we acknowledge, Christopher and Carolyn, who have taught us more about the importance of communication than any textbook can.

ABBREVIATIONS

APM	Association for Project Management
APM BoK	Association for Project Management Body of Knowledge
AQL	Acceptable Quality Level
BA	British Airways
BIS	business intelligence systems
BSI	British Standards Institution
CAD	computer aided design
CoIQ	cost of implementing quality
DSDM	dynamic systems development method
EDMS	engineering data management system
EFQM	European Foundation for Quality Management
EPA	US Environmental Protection Agency
IPMA	International Project Management Association
ISO	International Standards Organization
IT	Information Technology
KM	knowledge management
MIS	management Information systems
NASA	National Aeronautical and Space Administration (United States)
OAT	operational acceptance testing
OGC	UK Office of Government Commerce
OPM3	Organizational Project Management Maturity Model
P3M3	portfolio, programme and project management maturity model
PMI	Project Management Institute
PONC	price of non-conformance
PQM	project Quality Management
QMS	quality management system
RR	Rolls-Royce Ltd

xviii Abbreviations

SLA	service level agreement
SOPs	standard operating procedures
SPC	statistical process control
SRB	solid rocket booster
SSADM	structured systems analysis and design method
T5	Heathrow Airport Terminal 5
TQM	total quality management
TCO	total cost of ownership
TPIA	third party inspection authority
US NRC	United States Nuclear Regulatory Commission

1
WHAT IS QUALITY, AND WHY DO PRIORITIES NEED BALANCING?

A project that delivers an outcome that is not fit for purpose has failed, even if it is on time and budget. Subsequent work to make it fit for purpose, in order to realise its target business benefits, results in delays and additional costs.

In many cases, tight focus on managing project schedule or budget, to the detriment of quality, leads to project deliverables which are not fit for purpose, or which don't fully meet the requirements. Project Management Institute research (PMI, 2015) indicates between 11 per cent and 25 per cent of project spend is wasted globally, and this percentage is probably much higher for IT projects. Although project success rates are improving, 78 per cent of projects are at least partial failures according to the APM's research report (APM, 2015), and represent major wasted expenditure.

Virtually all project managers will be familiar with the 'iron' or 'golden' triangle, originally devised by Dr Martin Barnes CBE, former President of the Association for Project Management (APM), which characterises the priority-balancing challenges of project management (Figure 1.1).

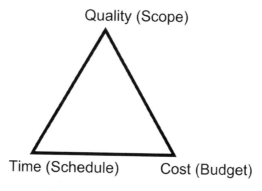

FIGURE 1.1 The iron triangle of project management

2 What is quality, and why do priorities need balancing?

There are variations on how the points of the triangle are labelled, but this version, with time, cost and quality, is the most fundamental. Dr Barnes devised this as a tool to allow project teams to discuss the trade-offs they were making and agree clear priorities for project completion. Techniques for managing both time and cost are well understood and comparatively straightforward (although not easy), but managing quality seems to get much less attention and has largely fallen out of fashion in project management literature.

This could be because:

1. In a period in which cost-cutting is the primary driver of government and large businesses, an understanding of what focusing on quality delivers, and why it is cost effective, has been lost by key decision makers preoccupied with cutting 'unnecessary cost'.
2. On large and complicated projects, responsibility for quality is delegated to specialist disciplines such as quality engineers, solutions architects, business analysts and systems engineers.
3. Expenditure and schedule are both easy to measure and set targets for; quality isn't (Atkinson, 1999).
4. Project management, as an emerging discipline, has focussed on commonality between projects. Techniques for establishing and maintaining control of the schedule and budget are cross-disciplinary. In contrast, techniques for controlling quality often require some specialist technical background knowledge, making general lessons on project quality more difficult to extract and articulate.

Attention to the different elements of the triangle needs to be balanced correctly to optimise project performance (detailed later in Section 1.7.1); projects that sacrifice quality to hit deadlines and budgets can easily fail. Heathrow Terminal 5's focus on opening on time and on budget led to a public relations disaster when the baggage handling system failed as a result of rushed testing and inadequate preparation.

The book sets out to apply author Rudyard Kipling's 'Six honest serving men' from his poem on enquiry:

- **What** is quality? – this chapter.
- **Why** manage quality? – Chapter 2.
- **Who** is responsible for quality? – Chapter 3.
- **When** does quality need managing? – Chapters 4 and 5.
- **Where** does quality need managing? – Chapter 6.
- **How** can quality be managed? – Chapters 7–12.

In recent years, what was once a single discipline of project management has been split into three; portfolio, programme and project management, and responsibilities for project success split between them. For the purposes of this book, this separation of responsibilities and disciplines has been set aside, and the single unified 'project management' discipline retained.

This chapter explores the different interpretations of the term 'quality', and concludes there are two subtly different definitions in the project context, 'fitness for purpose' and 'conformance to requirements' that must both be satisfied.

It goes on to review the development of quality management concepts and techniques in the manufacturing sector, before relating those concepts to project management, highlighting the differences between manufacturing and projects.

The need to balance the conflicting demands on a project is analysed, and as measuring is a key element of managing, the chapter then considers approaches to measuring quality in projects.

Learning outcomes for the chapter

After reading this chapter, the reader should understand:

1. Definitions of quality applicable to the project context.
2. Approaches to assessing quality.
3. The origins of quality management.
4. Why managing for quality must be balanced correctly against budget and schedule for each project.
5. Why quality can and should be quantified.

Project quality management (PQM) aims to ensure that the performance and benefits of the project outputs expected by the customer are delivered. It integrates all the project management activities needed to achieve this. This begs the question: what does 'quality' mean in the context of a project?

1.1 What does 'quality' mean?

Agreeing a definition of quality is fundamental to achieving it; without understanding what quality is, the project team cannot be expected to deliver it. A **shared** understanding of what it means in specific terms relating to the project environment and an **agreed** vocabulary of terms is needed.

In everyday usage, there is ambiguity around the word 'quality' – it is open to more than one interpretation. Just asking different people what it means to them will illustrate the variations in understanding of the term.

Here are some examples of products from everyday life that commonly attract the description 'quality':

- Country mansion.
- Louis Vuitton luggage.
- Rolex watch.

4 What is quality, and why do priorities need balancing?

In this sense, quality means luxurious or expensive.

An alternative list is:

- New three-bedroomed semi-detached house in the suburbs.
- Samsonite luggage.
- Seiko watch.

In this sense, 'quality' means well-designed and well-made at an affordable price. What most people would struggle with accepting as an example of 'quality' is the following list:

- Shack by the beach.
- Plastic carrier bag.
- Digital timer.

Yet each of these can be a quality product, when satisfying a particular set of needs.

> *Reflective exercise: what does the word 'quality' mean to you?*

1.2 Definitions of quality

Quality terms interpreted differently by different people will lead to misunderstandings. It is important within the project environment that everyone works to the same meanings, using the same terminology. The terminology within this book is based on the ISO 9000 family of standards relating to projects (see Chapter 11).

Definitions are available from several sources:

- The APM Body of Knowledge (APM 2012) says: 'Quality is broadly defined as fitness for purpose or more narrowly as the degree of conformance of the outputs and process [to requirements]'.
- PRINCE2®[1] says: [quality] products are fit for purpose. [They]:
  - Meet business expectations.
  - Enable the desired benefits to be achieved.
- BS EN ISO9000 (BSI, 2015) says quality results 'deliver value through fulfilling the needs and expectations of customers and other relevant interested parties'.

In the words of a popular television commercial, a quality product 'does what it says on the tin'.

Other leading authors on quality management have used the following definitions:

Crosby (1979): 'conformance to agreed and fully understood requirements'. Crosby's interpretation means that quality is not a sliding scale i.e. there is no such concept as high quality or low quality only 'conforming' and 'non-conforming'.

Juran (Juran and Godfrey, 2000): 'fitness for purpose/use'. This emphasises the quality aim of satisfying customer expectations and understanding both their needs and **future** requirements. It is the purchaser, customer or user that determines whether a product is fit for purpose.

Rose (2014) discusses alternative definitions at length, and concludes, 'Quality is the ability of a set of inherent characteristics of a product, system or process to fulfil requirements of customers and other interested partners'.

'Fitness for purpose' and 'conformance to requirements' have the same meaning only **if** the requirements referred to are completely understood, fully represent all of the requirements and have been documented accurately. Where the documented requirements are inaccurate, incomplete, emergent or inconsistent, 'conformance to requirements' can fail to achieve 'fitness for purpose'. A case of this is the pedestrian-induced resonant swing of the Millennium Bridge in London when it first opened.

In a project context, everyday meanings of the term 'Quality' must be set aside. So, project quality doesn't mean:

- Luxury i.e. an indulgence.
- Very high standards, excellence, 'fine'.
- Very expensive, high-priced, 'Gold-plated'.
- 'Better' than alternatives in some generic sense.

Juran and Godfrey (2000) stress that, in practice, 'over-specification' or including in the requirements more than is needed for the purpose, has adverse cost impacts and makes a 'right-first-time' product less likely.

'Grade' is a term that more accurately reflects common usage of the term quality, e.g. the higher the grade of a diamond, the fewer flaws, the better the colour, the lower the fluorescence etc. When choosing a diamond, however, its quality reflects its fitness for purpose: a high-grade diamond is a poor quality choice for cutting glass as it is far too expensive.

What 'quality' really means is best illustrated by some everyday examples.

1.3 Quality as 'meeting requirements'

Three everyday cases illustrate the relationship between 'quality' and requirements. These reflect three choices we may make as consumers or customers seeking quality.

If you are booking a flight to travel to a destination, what are your quality requirements and how do these influence your choice of carrier? Why does the cost of the flight vary so substantially between carriers? National 'flag carrier' airlines can offer some advantages and benefits for frequent fliers and passengers travelling on business. The same travellers may use low cost airlines for their personal and family journeys if their requirements are different.

Table 1.1 shows the sort of requirements which would make either type of carrier a good choice. The traveller's individual or corporate requirements define

6 What is quality, and why do priorities need balancing?

TABLE 1.1 Quality in choice of airlines

Flag Carrier Airline Quality airline if your requirements are:	*Low-cost Airline* Quality airline if your requirements are:
• First Class or Business Class • Lay-flat seating for sleep • High levels of care included • Benefits for frequent fliers • Extensive route network • Robustness to air traffic congestion • Business Lounge at airport • Typically, destination close to city centres • Networking opportunities • Changeable flight ticket	• Low fares • Adequate comfort for flight times • Additional services available on the flight at affordable prices • Public airport facilities only • Route network may be more convenient for holiday destinations • Punctuality is not critical • Ability to change flights not critical • Ability to rest or work on journey not needed

what is meant by 'quality'. In selecting a flight, delivering 'quality' for a business trip may lead to a different solution to 'quality' for a week's holiday. Travel agents know that the customer needs to be asked about their requirements to deliver an acceptable solution.

At the airport, on the way to your destination, you may decide to go shopping in the duty-free area. Perhaps you need a bag to take with you as you anticipate doing a lot of walking and need a way to transport your belongings. A small rucksack from a reputable manufacturer may seem appealing. Why spend money on the rucksack when you could just pick up a plastic bag from the duty-free shop and use that instead?

The perception of 'quality' and the customer's requirements can be considered in the choice of bag. Consider what requirements would cause you to buy a rucksack from a reputable manufacturer, and when you would choose to use a reusable carrier bag. Table 1.2 shows the sort of requirements you would have for either of these to be a good choice; your requirements define whether they are 'quality' for you.

On arrival, you need a way to get from the airport to your destination. You will have considered this decision before setting off and arrangements will hopefully

TABLE 1.2 Quality in choice of bags

Brand Name Rucksack Quality bag if:	*Plastic bag* Quality bag if:
• Functionality is important • Weather resistance is important • Longevity is required • Cost is of secondary importance	• Basic functionality only required • Longevity is not required • Cost is main driver

What is quality, and why do priorities need balancing? **7**

TABLE 1.3 Quality in choice of cars

Executive Limousine A quality car if your requirements are:	*Mass-produced Estate* A quality car if your requirements are:
• Demonstrating status (prestige) • Work required in transit (chauffeur-driven) • Cost of little concern • Fuel economy of little concern • Comfort a major factor	• Economy • Reliability • Reasonably comfortable • Lots of luggage space • Self-drive • Prestige not a major issue

be in place. Consider what requirements would cause you to hire a limousine, and when you would hire a mass-produced estate car. Table 1.3 shows the sort of requirements you would have for either of these to be a good choice; your requirements define whether they are 'quality' for you.

So, setting requirements and making choices based on our perception of quality, is something that we do in everyday life. It is also something that retailers and service providers are very much aware of as they seek to establish their reputation as quality providers.

1.4 A brief history of quality management

Since the start of manufacturing, manufacturers have sought to improve quality levels in their products. The discipline of quality management is rooted in the early days of manufacturing industry (Juran, 1995) when the role of quality control inspector arose. Statistical analysis of quality data collected during the manufacturing process started in the 1920s and, in 1924, Schewart introduced the first control chart. These developments eventually led to the introduction of statistical process control (SPC), although this was not for some time widely adopted in manufacturing industry. During the Second World War, American munitions factories became much more interested in quality management due to the need to increase manufacturing quality and effectiveness to support the war effort. The focus here was on manufacturing consistency, cutting rework and waste.

After the Second World War, the new generation of quality experts saw the acceptance of production wastage as planning to fail, and strongly advocated the principles of 'right first time' and 'zero defects'. Initially, US factories were slow to take up the quality initiatives developed in the munitions plants. However, this was not the case in Japan, where support from American quality consultants, notably Joseph Juran, W. Edwards Deming and Armand Feigenbaum, was readily accepted to help war-decimated industries recover.

Quality management practices grew rapidly in Japanese factories from the early 1950s. By the late 1960s, this transformed Japanese products from cheap but poor imitations to both cheap and high quality. In 1969, Feigenbaum presented the concept of 'total quality' for the first time, at the first International Conference on

8 What is quality, and why do priorities need balancing?

Quality Control in Tokyo. This encompassed not only quality control of materials and production output, but also much wider aspects such as planning, organisation and management responsibility. A key principle recognised was that all levels in an organisation, from top to bottom, must adopt quality management.

This revolution in quality management slowly spread to the West. Total quality management (TQM) started to gather momentum in the UK during the early 1980s and this accelerated when Japanese companies started opening factories in Britain, such as the Nissan plant in Washington, Tyne and Wear, and the Sony television plant in South Wales.

TQM forms a foundation of current enterprise wide concepts such as Lean Thinking and Six Sigma, influencing the thinking of both organisational and project management (Oakland and Marosszeky, 2017).

1.4.1 How does quality management in projects differ from in manufacturing?

Due to its birth in manufacturing, most writing and thought about quality management is about manufacturing and products. The challenge is to transfer these insights from manufacturing and products into project management, (project) deliverables/outputs and (programme) outcomes.

Key differences between quality management in the project context and the manufacturing context include:

- The number of times the 'product' is produced is very much smaller in projects than in manufacturing; often the outputs from the project are 'one offs'. This means that quality in projects does not have the same focus on 'repeatability' as in manufacturing.
- In a project environment, there are fewer opportunities to 'learn from experience' and incrementally improve outputs. Getting it right first time is important due to the small number of repetitions.
- Where there **are** repeated similar outputs, usually the time taken to produce the first one is a large fraction of the project timescale – by the time the lesson is learned, there is little time left to apply it.
- High levels of complexity in the project and lack of familiarity creates uncertainty in what is needed to produce quality.

These key differences prevent many manufacturing-orientated quality management techniques being carried over directly to project management.

Small numbers of repeated events preclude the direct use of statistical techniques such as statistical process control. 'Continuous improvement' is difficult to apply within a project as the period within which an activity is taking place in generally quite short. Learning from experience within a project can only be reused if activities are repeated. If there are no repeat activities, the benefits of learning are only harvested if that learning can be shared with the rest of the projects in

What is quality, and why do priorities need balancing? **9**

the organisation. This puts the responsibility for 'continuous improvement' and extracting lessons learned with the project, programme or portfolio management office.

The incremental learning from experience and gradual evolution of processes, as embodied in most manufacturing quality improvement approaches, is not generally applicable to projects. Applying quality management to projects requires planning and prevention rather than improvement. There is an emphasis on thinking ahead – how to get it right first time, rather than the fourth or fifth time. **Planning** and **risk management** are the two most obvious 'forward-looking' disciplines of project management – these need to work extra-hard to prevent quality problems.

Use of 'pilot' projects and breaking down large projects into incremental stages can be beneficial in achieving quality results. In a successful telecoms billing project, a decision was taken to pilot a customer migration at an early stage of the project. This allowed the lessons learned to be incorporated, and the project then steadily increased the scale and complexity of delivery at subsequent stages of the project to reach a successful outcome, as described in Case study 1.

CASE STUDY 1: CRITICAL SUCCESS CRITERIA DRIVING PROJECT APPROACH

Telecoms company A had acquired company B and after six months had successfully integrated most aspects of the business. However, the progress they had made in moving to a unified billing system had stalled. Since maintaining the legacy systems inherited from company B was expensive, the company wanted to migrate company B's users onto the same systems used by the customers of company A. Figure 1.2 illustrates the operational rationalisation and large cost savings of billing integration.

From interviewing the project's sponsor, the critical success measure was customer retention. This type of project is notorious for making customers so unhappy that they change supplier. The perceived high risk of losing customers had led to a resistance to change and the migration project stalling. Once retention of customers was recognised as the primary requirement, the project approach was changed to make the main objective giving a good customer experience. This was a major shift in thinking for the project team, whose previous focus had been on the IT aspects.

After extensive scoping analysis, it became clear that there were at least six different business viewpoints, reflecting the interests of different functions within the business, each with different people involved. The team engaged all those parts of the business in a small pilot, the simplest they could conceive. Within three months, they successfully transferred 50 customers with very simple service holdings. In doing this, they learned many things about

10   What is quality, and why do priorities need balancing?

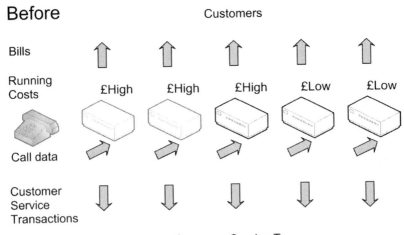

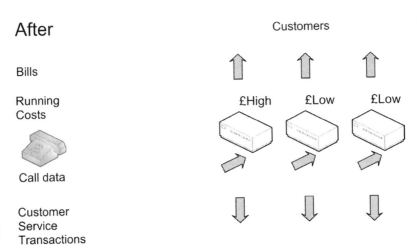

FIGURE 1.2 Convergence of billing systems and consequent operating cost savings

managing the customer experience, and planned the following phase to cover more complex service holdings and a larger group of customers.

Progressing incrementally in this way, they were able to give a good customer experience, manage risk effectively, stay within budget and hit the target date for the project. The client was delighted that customer loss from the project was negligible.

1.5 Quality management in the project context

According to PRINCE2 (2009), Quality Management is 'the co-ordinated activities to direct and control an organisation with regard to quality'.

The APM BoK (APM, 2012) defines project quality management as 'the discipline that is applied to ensure that both the outputs of the project and the processes by which the outputs are delivered meet the required needs of stakeholders'.

The requirements of the project, together with the acceptance criteria for the outputs (in measurable terms), come together as the starting point for project quality management.

Quality management involves the following processes (APM, 2012):

1. Quality planning – defines how the requirements will be met while balancing the cost and timing trade-offs.
2. Quality assurance – aims to **prevent** defects before they happen.
3. Quality control – aims to **detect** defects after they have happened.
4. Continuous improvement – learning from mistakes to reduce future defects.

These four processes are also the key elements of TQM (see Chapter 4) and aim to achieve results both efficiently and effectively.

There are two important concepts related to the full life of the project outputs that influence project delivery. Ideally, they are captured in the Project Business Case, but if not, they lie outside the project's direct remit. These are:

- **Economic lifetime** – the expected period of time during which an asset is useful to the average owner, generating a viable return on investment.
- **Total cost of ownership (TCO)** – the total cost estimate for creating, maintaining and operating an asset for its economic lifetime.

These are key factors in deciding what makes the output fit for purpose; a dam that crumbles after 10 years, or a warship gearbox that needs replacing every six months may be quick and cheap to deliver initially, but are unlikely to meet the requirements.

Division of responsibilities across project teams means that some conflict of interest is inherent between those responsible for:

- Controlling costs.
- Meeting timescales.
- Delivering a fit-for-purpose solution meeting the requirements.

There may well be a lack of shared understanding, between the project team members and the project sponsor and stakeholders, as to acceptable trade-offs between time, cost and quality. It is vitally important to create a shared

12 What is quality, and why do priorities need balancing?

understanding of what constitutes 'quality' in terms of the project and this is an essential element of project success.

1.6 Measuring quality

Having defined what quality is, and given the need to assess it in an objective way to manage it effectively, what measures can be used that align with the quality targets?

1.6.1 Setting quality targets

In managing quality, it is very important to set clear and realistic targets for what needs to be achieved. Historically, it was usual to have manufacturing targets which allowed a proportion of the output as scrap. If these targets were met, the manufacturing process or project was seen as successful.

In the early 20th century, the Royal Navy procured shells for its guns and applied a very poor acceptance testing policy. A small sample of the shells from each batch was tested, and if the sample passed the test criteria then the batch was accepted. If the sample failed, the batch was rejected BUT could be resubmitted by the manufacturer for retesting. In practice, shell batches were resubmitted and retested until, through luck, a sample passed and the remaining shells were accepted. The consequence of this is that the failure rate of the shells finally supplied was well above the standard required. In action, the Royal Navy's ships were placed at a serious disadvantage when the shells they fired at the Battle of Jutland failed to perform (McCallum, 2003, 2004, 2005).

Defects cost the project time, money and stakeholder confidence. Adopting a policy of 'right first time' and removing acceptance of failure, drives planning for success, even if perfection isn't achieved.

Where the project is in difficulty and the quality, time and cost constraints cannot be satisfied, something must be sacrificed. Commonly, this involves reducing testing, changes to project scope and/or accepting outputs of reduced capability to meet schedule and budget. Experience suggests that an honest discussion with the client will reveal that there is more flexibility in time or cost than there is in quality, especially if good stakeholder management builds a trusted relationship between client and project.

1.6.2 Qualitative quality assessment

In everyday life, assessments of quality are frequently qualitative themselves i.e. descriptive rather than measurable. People talk about something being of 'excellent' quality, 'good' quality or 'poor' quality.

The problem with qualitative terms is that they cannot be measured, so assessment is subjective. This can lead to serious disagreements and confusion, especially in a contractual situation.

1.6.3 Quantitative quality assessment

Quantitative measures of quality avoid these issues, as they **are** measurable, and objective.

Historically, the quantitative measure of quality has been the Acceptable Quality Level (AQL, BS 4778, 1991), the acceptable proportion of out-of-tolerance items. This is a definition relating to repeated production; for project purposes it is not useful. A project is working towards a unique output (or a handful of outputs) and cannot afford the time and cost of discovering some deliverables are not fit for purpose.

A quality target of **right first time** means a zero tolerance for products being unfit for purpose. **'Zero defects'** as a literal target i.e. every product is flawless, is rarely practicable in reality; much of what is performed in a construction project, for instance, is highly dependent on manual processes that cannot be controlled as tightly as machining processes. Manual welding, brick laying and painting are as much an art as a science, and so some level of flaws are acceptable within the quality limits defined but the **aim** should be to avoid them.

As well as the AQL, there are many other numerical measures of quality such as standard deviation of the measured value, and defect rate (e.g. occurrences per 1,000,000). In IT projects, quality is assessed through such measures as number of defects identified and system downtime.

Specific metrics are discussed later in this book, however the key metric for measuring quality is not just the number or proportion of defects or reported errors but the **price of non-conformance or PONC** (Crosby, 1979). PONC is also referred to as the cost of non-quality.

1.6.4 The price of non-conformance (or cost of failure)

The price of non-conformance (PONC) is the cost to the project of **all the ramifications** of a quality target not being achieved i.e. something being provided that is not fit for purpose. These costs can be widespread and significant, and may well include:

- Wasted effort in discovering the problem and subsequent retests.
- Delay costs to the project, often not covered by contractual agreements.
- Damage to working relationships with subcontractors if liquidated damages are invoked.
- Rework costs, which may be entirely borne by the subcontractor, but which reduce their opportunity to profit from the work and in severe cases may even drive the subcontractor out of business.
- Loss of business benefits due to delayed commissioning.
- Safety compromise, leading to injury or death.

Achieving quality is not free; there is always some cost associated with it. Against the price of non-conformance must be weighed the cost of designing and building

14 What is quality, and why do priorities need balancing?

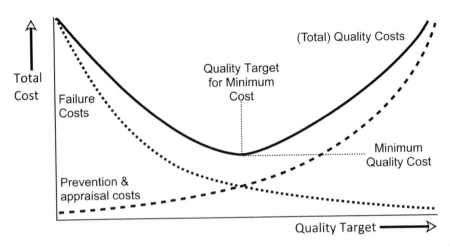

FIGURE 1.3 The trade-off between the cost of achieving quality and the cost of failing to

for quality, and the costs of validating requirements and verifying at the earliest opportunity that they have all been met. These costs of implementing quality can be substantial and are **certain**. In contrast, as non-conformance is only a **possibility**, the price of non-conformance must take into account its **likelihood**. This gives a trade-off between the **cost** of preventing non-conformance and the **price** of non-conformance (failure costs). The principle of this trade-off, and overall optimum, are illustrated in Figure 1.3.

Car insurance is an everyday illustration of a similar trade-off – the driver routinely pays the **certain** cost of insurance premiums, analogous to the cost of implementing quality (including prevention and appraisal costs), to avoid meeting the **potential** huge cost of accident and damage, analogous to the price of non-conformance. The driver considers that it is worth paying a regular premium so that **if the event occurs**, the insurance company will reimburse the much greater loss. The insurance company is aware of the probability of the event occurring, so sets the premium according to the risk. Young, inexperienced driver face a high premium until they have proven their safety record, so the trade-off between affordability of the premium and level of cover is often challenging for them.

In many projects, the minimum overall cost is determined by high quality standards as the price of non-conformance is so high, e.g. in the nuclear industry a leak can be very costly indeed. This is illustrated in Figure 1.4 – the higher the quality target of the project (the fewer defects created, the fewer concessions allowed suppliers for not meeting acceptable standards, the greater the investment in 'right first time') the greater the cost of implementing quality, but the lower the risk of non-conformance, so the lower the likely cost of failure.

Suppliers need to factor in their own costs to their price for delivery to particular quality standards, and the customer should be prepared to pay a premium to reduce

What is quality, and why do priorities need balancing? 15

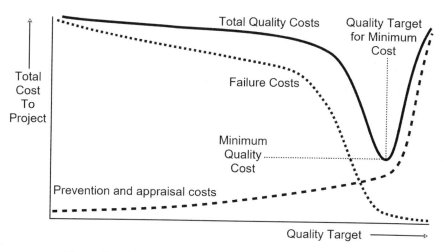

FIGURE 1.4 The trade-off between the cost of achieving quality and the cost of failing to, in projects

the price of non-conformance. The net benefit is still positive if quality management is effective.

The need to take the price of non-conformance into account, rather than purchase cost alone was brought home to a major oil and gas company when their procurement team sourced a cheaper component for a model of deep-sea oil wellhead. Buying the lower-specification components saved $10 each, but when they failed, each cost over $100 million to replace!

1.7 Conclusions of chapter

There are two subtly different definitions in the project context, 'fitness for purpose' and 'conformance to requirements' that must **both** be satisfied for project success.

Developed in the manufacturing sector, quality management concepts must be adapted significantly for the project environment to deal with its different challenges.

As measuring is a key element of managing, measuring quality in projects is necessary, and the price of non-conformance is the key measure of quality.

Note

1. PRINCE2® is a registered trademark of AXELOS Limited. All rights reserved.

1.8 Bibliography

APM (2012) 'APM Body of Knowledge', 6th edition, Association for Project Management, ISBN: 978-1-903494-40-0

APM Research Report (2015) 'Conditions for Project Success', APM

Atkinson, R. (1999) 'Project management: cost, time and quality, two best guesses and a phenomenon, it's time to accept other success criteria', International Journal of Project Management 17:6, 337–42

BS 4778 (1991) 'BS 4778-3.1:1991 Quality vocabulary. Availability, reliability and maintainability terms. Guide to concepts and related definitions', British Standards Institution, ISBN: 0580197530

BSI (2015) 'BS EN ISO 9000:2015 Quality management systems, Fundamentals and Vocabulary', British Standards Institution, ISBN: 9780580788789

BSI (2015a), 'BS EN ISO 9001:2015 Quality management systems. Requirements', British Standards Institution, ISBN: 9780580918162

BSI (2009) 'BS EN ISO 9004:2009 Managing for the sustained success of an organisation. A quality management approach', British Standards Institution, ISBN: 9780580555237

BSI (2003) 'BS ISO 10006:2003 Quality management systems. Guidelines for quality management in projects', British Standards Institution, ISBN: 0580421686

Crosby, P.B. (1979) 'Quality is Free: The Art of Making Quality Certain', McGraw-Hill, New York, ISBN: 9780451625854

Juran, J.M. (Editor) (1995) 'A History of Managing for Quality' First edition, Irwin Professional Publishing, ISBN: 9780873893411

Juran, J.M. and Godfrey, B. (2000) 'Juran's Quality Control Handbook', 5th edition, McGraw-Hill, New York, ISBN: 9780071165396

McCallum, I. (2003) 'The Riddle of the Shells, 1914–18: The Approach to War, 1882–1914', Warship 2002–2003, Ed. Antony Preston, Conway Maritime Press, pp. 3–25, ISBN: 0851779263

McCallum, I. (2004) 'The Riddle of the Shells, 1914–18: Part Two: The Test of Battle, Heligoland to the Dardanelles', Warship 2004, Ed. Antony Preston, Conway Maritime Press, pp. 9–20, ISBN: 0851779484

McCallum, I. (2005) 'The Riddle of the Shells, 1914–18: Part Three: Disappointment in the North Sea', Warship 2005, Ed. Antony Preston; John Jordan, Conway Maritime Press, pp. 9–24, ISBN: 1844860035

Oakland, J.S. and Marosszeky, M. (2017) 'Total Construction Management Lean Quality in Construction Project Delivery', Taylor and Francis, ISBN: 9781317439325

PMI (2015) 'Taking a Pulse infographic 2015' https://www.pmi.org/learning/thought-leadership/pulse

PRINCE2 (2009) 'Managing Successful Projects with PRINCE2' 2009 edition, Axelos Ltd, ISBN: 9780113310593

Rose, K. (2014) 'Project Quality Management: Why, What and How', 2nd edition, J Ross Publishing, ISBN: 9781604271027

2

WHY MANAGE QUALITY?

'Finishing on time and within budget is not much consolation if the result of a project does not work' (PRINCE2, 2009)

This chapter covers the benefits of producing deliverables that are fit for purpose and conform to requirements, illustrating this with case studies, and exploring how striking the right balance of focus between time, cost and quality impacts on project success, including reductions in cost and time.

It explains how failure to meet appropriate quality targets creates delays and cost overruns, and how investment in getting the quality right results in benefits to both schedule and budget.

It considers the special challenges facing major engineering projects, and analyses them, drawing out how quality failures can have significant financial and safety implications.

It then recommends an approach to justifying investment in quality for a portfolio, programme or large project, balancing the focus between cost, time and quality appropriately.

Learning outcomes for the chapter

After reading this chapter, the reader should understand how:

1. Good project quality management enhances safety.
2. Good project quality management reduces delays.
3. Good project quality management controls costs.
4. Good project quality management enhances customer satisfaction.
5. Investment in improving quality can be justified in quantitative and financial terms.

18 Why manage quality?

2.1 What are the benefits of effective quality management?

The principal benefits of good quality management are:

1. Improved safety.
2. Improved timeliness.
3. Controlled cost.
4. Customer satisfaction (even delight).
5. Increased commercial success.
6. Increased project morale.

These are well illustrated by a project that was very effective in its quality management, delivering success against all criteria despite enormous technical challenges – the Rion-Antirion Bridge. The Rion-Antirion Bridge Case study (Case study 2, included in full in the Appendix) results from interviewing the deputy project manager during a visit to the bridge, supplemented by details from the Institute of Civil Engineers (ICE, online).

> ### CASE STUDY 2: GETTING THE BALANCE RIGHT – RION-ANTIRION BRIDGE
>
> The Rion-Antirion Bridge crosses the Gulf of Corinth in Greece. Figure 2.1 shows the whole span of the bridge.
>
> Design challenges included strong winds, deep water, no secure foundations, and major earthquake activity. It is presented as an example of a project quality success because:
>
> - It won the International Association for Bridge and Structural Engineering's Outstanding Structure Award.
> - It was completed four months early, earning a large bonus.
> - It was completed within budget tolerance.
> - There were no fatalities during this project.
> - It has survived all subsequent earthquakes, as designed.
>
> How was this achieved? Quality was a focus of the project team from the start.
>
>
>
> **FIGURE 2.1** Rion-Antirion Bridge (Photograph © Andrew Wright)

Why manage quality? **19**

- Requirements: time was spent on making sure that the requirements were clear and well documented.
- Leadership: technical focus rather than financial focus applied, looking for solutions to problems, not blame attribution.
- Standards, disciplines and processes: clear and imposed from the start of the project.
- Organisation: designed at the start; quality roles and responsibilities clearly defined.
- Design: designed for quality from the start, with all drawings in the central Engineering Data Management system (EDMS) under strict change control.
- Change control: rigorously applied, with change management responsiveness targets included in the project's key performance indicators.
- Quality Methods: were all best practice. Independent inspection authorities were used.
- Team building: sub-contractor problems were shared by the project team, who helped to overcome the problems rather than criticise.
- Continuity from construction to maintenance: many construction workers stayed on after completion to operate and maintain the bridge.
- Safety: short safety workshops every two weeks meant no fatalities on the project.
- 'Green' waste and energy management were designed into the project
- Strong risk management:
  1. The need for dampers on stay cables – fittings were built in cheaply as mitigation, but the expensive dampers were only bought and fitted when the need was proven.
  2. Simple expansion joints, replaced after any strong earthquake, were chosen as a more cost-effective solution than earthquake-proof designs.
- Pragmatic issue management: when the first pylon was sunk into place, its location was 200mm outside tolerance. The project team adjusted the design of the bridge rather than move the pylon.

This Case study is a clear example of how putting quality first resulted in project success, meeting schedule and budget constraints. These disciplines are applicable to all projects.

The benefits are now considered in more detail.

2.1.1 Improved safety through quality management

Safety is a key requirement for all projects, so any safety failure is, by definition, a quality failure. Quality failures can also create safety issues. Treating quality with less rigour than safety can result in safety implications being underestimated, leading

20 Why manage quality?

to tragedy. The Space Shuttle Columbia Case study (3) shows how a project's quality failure resulted in the death of seven US astronauts.

CASE STUDY 3: SAFETY – SPACE SHUTTLE COLUMBIA – ADAPTED FROM NASA (2003)

On 1 February 2003, Shuttle Orbiter *Columbia* burnt-up during re-entry, killing all seven crew. Each space mission is a project; this one was a lethal failure.

The loss of *Columbia* was caused by foam insulation falling from the external tank during take-off, smashing into the leading edge of the left wing and punching a hole in it. During re-entry, this hole allowed superheated air to enter the wing, causing its collapse and the catastrophic breakup of the Shuttle.

Foam shedding and debris strikes were forbidden by the original specification, but NASA found they occurred in service. As no practical solution was found, NASA eventually accepted them as a risk. Just two launches before Columbia's loss, a foam strike made a large dent in the casing of a solid rocket booster. Despite this, NASA elected to continue with their launch programme.

The strike during Columbia's launch was observed by closed circuit television monitoring, and while still in orbit, NASA managers suspected damage. They limited their investigation, however; they decided to estimate the possible damage instead of inspecting the actual damage directly (by telescope or spacewalk). The damage-prediction software used, based on testing with ice pieces, predicted severe damage, including penetration of multiple tiles and possibly the wing leading edge too. However, NASA engineers believed that the less dense foam would do less damage than ice. NASA managers accepted this fallacious reasoning, convincing themselves that only slight damage to the wing could have occurred.

The vehicle suffered serious damage because the foam insulation wasn't **fit for purpose** – a piece falling from the main tank was directly responsible for the critical damage. **Conformance to requirements** had been compromised; no cure for foam shedding had been applied, despite the clear requirement. The compromise to project quality due to time and budget constraints, had tragic results.

2.1.2 Improved cost control through quality management

There are direct impacts on project duration, costs and benefits from failure to hit quality targets i.e. the outcome is not fit for purpose, and/or doesn't meet customer requirements.

Quality in rework avoidance: where a product fails to satisfy its acceptance tests, the rework required to fix the problem not only costs money but also creates a delay. It may be the supplier's problem **but** it is also the project's problem. Additional duration results in extra man-hours being funded by the project because many of the staff cannot simply be 'switched off'; their costs continue to be incurred.

If there is any contractual ambiguity, there is a reasonable chance that the supplier will try to negotiate the sharing of the rework costs, causing delays which put pressure on the project to accept the additional cost; the longer the delay for negotiating, the greater the delay cost to the project will be. Some major projects have come to a standstill, incurring enormous additional costs, due to contractual discussions e.g. cessation of work on the Channel Tunnel due to contractual disputes between TML (the contractor) and Eurotunnel (the owner).

Adding together the loss of business benefit and increased project costs can quickly destroy a project's business case, and make success impossible. Getting things right from the start avoids these problems – minimising rework and retest will reduce the cost of the project significantly.

Contractual ambiguity around handling quality issues is a project quality management failure in its own right.

Quality in cost escalation avoidance: contractors are often pressured by economic circumstances to bid for work at a very low profit margin to cover their fixed costs. A common way to increase this margin involves change notes or contract variations which are more profitable than the original contract. Such contractual variations can create huge increases in the total cost of the work through arguing effectively that the customer requires something different to what they ordered.

Understanding what is required is essential to placing accurate orders with suppliers, and if an accurate requirement cannot be determined before order placement, the type of contract used must reflect the certainty of change, and the high level of risk.

Setting up appropriate project contracts is a key element of project quality management.

2.1.3 Improved timeliness – delay avoidance – through quality management

The consequences of delays to projects fall into to two major categories:

- Loss of business benefit due to delayed project completion.
- Increasing project costs due to rework and longer engagement of project staff.

In an ideal world, there would be no delays to the project; everything would arrive on time and would fit perfectly. However, there is always risk and uncertainty which can affect the project duration.

As the Rion-Antirion Bridge Case study illustrates, eradicating the delays due to problems with quality can substantially improve delivery to plan, holding down project costs to within budget.

Figure 2.2 indicates how additional preparation for quality can lead to finishing earlier. Early investment in quality planning delays the start of execution, however

Why manage quality?

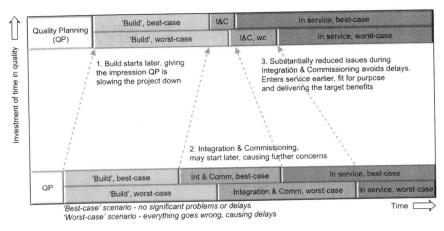

FIGURE 2.2 Trade-off between quality planning and project delay reduction

this investment in quality assurance pays back through reducing the delays in testing, commissioning and acceptance, more than making up for the later start. Careful prioritisation of long lead-time critical-path products may result in little or no delay to starting execution.

Figure 2.2 aims to show the uncertainty in timelines that results from defects and rework. The best case (BC) timescale reflects the minimum time, resulting from no significant defects, and the worst case (WC) timescale results from extensive rework caused by defects.

Early quality planning may delay the start of execution, but will result in worst case (WC) timelines closer to the best case, leading to earlier delivery. Skimping on quality planning, jumping quickly into execution, is likely to result in a higher level of defects, and longer worst case (WC) timescales, likely causing late completion and cost overruns.

The value of early quality analysis and planning is illustrated by Ralph R Young (Young, 2003), who reported that: 'Project cost statistics at the Cost & Economic Analysis Branch, National Aeronautics and Space Administration headquarters indicate that projects that spent less than 5 per cent of total project or program costs on the requirements process experienced an 80 per cent to 200 per cent cost overrun, whereas those that invested per cent to 14 per cent experienced less than a 60 per cent overrun'.

2.1.4 Customer satisfaction through quality management

Good quality usually satisfies, or even delights, the customer, even if there is some budget or time overrun. 'The bitterness of poor quality remains long after the sweetness of low price is forgotten' is attributed both to Benjamin Franklin and to Aldo Gucci, and 'The quality will remain long after the price is forgotten' to Sir Henry Royce.

The APM BoK (APM, 2012) states: *'Project success is the satisfaction of stakeholder needs and is measured by the success criteria as identified and agreed at the start of the project.* **From the project manager's perspective success may mean meeting agreed scope, time, cost and quality objectives'.**

This definition is debatable – some successful projects fail to hit their initial targets but deliver benefits beyond expectations, and some projects hit their targets but are rated failures because they deliver benefits below expectation. This identifies a key element of quality management, the alignment of requirements and customer expectations **at the end of the project**. Although overdelivering is not always a good thing, under-promising and over-delivering is by far preferable (and more likely to delight the customer), than over-promising and under-delivering.

Quality planning needs to take into account the project's target benefits and how they will be quantified, tracked and managed (even though they may not be realised until sometime after handover) **as the benefits are the reason for doing the project** and their eventual delivery forms the over-arching requirement, and the basis for customer satisfaction.

Experience suggests that customer–supplier relationships generally work better in partnership than conflict. If both partners are striving to deliver on time, on budget, while meeting quality requirements, then the probability of the project being a success is appreciably higher than when the customer and supplier are working towards different goals. Managing quality is critical to achieving a shared understanding, with everyone working towards the same outcome.

When it becomes clear during a project that there is a misunderstanding with a commercial impact, it puts a strain on the relationship. Ideally, as soon as a misunderstanding is recognised then both parties will work together to resolve it and move the project forward. When a misunderstanding is not discovered until late on, there will be substantial costs involved in correcting the situation and blame is allocated, forcing both parties to pay close attention to their respective interests. Conflicting interests can result in the engagement of legal professionals and contract experts, whose painstaking work can cause further delays. This makes rebuilding an effective working relationship even more difficult.

There is a multiplying effect on the value of quality; the value lost through a supplier's quality failings is **all** the work the disappointed customer would have placed with them in the future.

Quality and liability

If quality failures lead to a catastrophic problem, the potential cost can massively outweigh any savings made by cutting corners.

The liability for quality failures rests with a project's customer, but they can justifiably share that with any supplier whose work contributed to failure where there was provable negligence. If the customer has provided a clear set of requirements to the supplier, and they provide a solution that doesn't meet the requirements, the

24 Why manage quality?

supplier is liable for the consequences of failure. Where the customer requests a specific product, they remain liable if that product isn't fit for purpose.

Quality management affects everyone, just like safety. If quality management is seen within the organisation as being the responsibility of a select set of people only, it will fail.

Case study 4 shows how the failure to set up a new manufacturing facility to make fit-for-purpose engine components risked the lives of hundreds of passengers, resulted in substantial liability payments and damaged the reputation of Rolls-Royce as an engine supplier.

CASE STUDY 4: TRENT ENGINE MANUFACTURING CHANGES

On 4 November 2010, a Qantas Airbus A380 suffered a serious failure of one of its Rolls-Royce (RR) Trent 972 engines. An oil fire from a fractured pipe in the turbine area of the engine caused disintegration of a turbine disc, which spat out three fragments causing severe damage to the airframe, control systems and fuel system. The aircraft lost use of the wing slats, increasing landing speed. The loss of throttle control to one otherwise-undamaged engine meant it remained at cruise thrust during and after landing. The strong leadership of the aircraft captain and effective team working on the flight deck led to a safe landing.

Luckily, no one was injured, but the estimated cost of repairing the damaged aircraft was Aus$139 million and Qantas grounded its six A380s for over three weeks. The damaged aircraft was out of revenue-earning service for 18 months. RR paid Qantas Aus$95 million (£62 million) in settlement, and the Emergency Airworthiness Directive, requiring frequent and stringent tests, caused substantial cost to all operators of these engines.

The subsequent investigation found that the failure was due to out-of-tolerance oil feed pipes in the engine. This was due to failure to set up adequate production and quality control checks when engine manufacturing was re-located.

(Adapted from the final accident investigation report – ATSB, 2010.)

2.1.5 Delivering commercial benefits through quality

Chapter 1 considered how too great a focus on cost cutting early in the project could compromise quality, potentially reducing the chances of project success. Turning this on its head, is effective quality management likely to deliver commercial benefits?

Looking at **quality in general, not just the project context**, there are strong commercial benefits reported by Sargeant et al (2012):

Why manage quality? **25**

- Improved revenue – key reason; quality products and services sell well, at a premium price.
- Improved profit margins – these result from improved prices and control of costs.
- Customer loyalty – good handling of issues increases loyalty, turning customers into advocates.

The factors considered by members of the public when buying a product, in descending order of importance (from a study by Gallup for the American Society for Quality, Ryan, 1988 and Hutchens, 1989), are:

- Performance.
- Durability and reliability.
- Cost.
- Styling and branding.

People pay more for what they believe is a quality product; they are paying for peace of mind.

Paul McLoughlin, Managing Director Sixt Car Rental ('Director Magazine', 2011) said:

'Competing on price only is a dangerous strategy. People will pay for convenience, great customer service, and brands they adhere to.'

> *Reflective exercise: in the project environment, you have to make the case for the value of 'quality' over 'the cheapest possible' to people who in their private lives recognise the value of quality, why is that – how many directors fly in the cheapest seats or drive the cheapest cars?*

If quality is associated with commercial performance, improvements in quality management support, rather than damage, profitability.

We have often observed that some managers and staff see quality improvement as an **alternative** to improving the financial or productivity aspects of their work, with time and effort invested in developing quality simply as being lost to delivery. This view is misguided because effort invested in producing products right first time has the benefits of reducing wastage, rework and customer complaints.

Studying winners of TQM awards in the US, Hendricks and Singhal (1996) found the winners:

- Experienced an increase in operating income that was double that of their peers.
- Achieved sales growth more than double that of their peers.
- Increased their number of employees.
- Substantially outperformed the market average over the five years of the study.

26 Why manage quality?

Quality drives confidence, so is less negotiable than either price or delivery timescales. If an order, contract or customer is lost through poor quality the chances of recovering it are significantly lower than if lost through price or time (Dale et al, 2016).

Dale and Lascelles (Dale et al, 2007) found that developing a culture of quality management shows an increasing benefit, but warns that there are no quick wins – benefits are reaped from sustained quality improvement only, with the benefits rising exponentially with perseverance; short-term initiatives don't deliver; persistence is needed.

Two decades on from some of the original studies, the world has changed, with the banking crisis, recession and disruptive use of technology all changing markets quickly and undermining established businesses. The pressure to deliver change quickly and cheaply has risen, **but** projects are only successful if they deliver what is needed. Paradoxically, these pressures have increased the need for delivering right first time, so good project quality management still results in improved commercial performance.

2.1.6 Increased project morale

Personal experience shows that working in a quality way is a win-win, and personally satisfying. It minimises conflict of interest, resulting in happier and more motivated staff and overall improvement in productivity, we have found.

Google have a great reputation for their employees' standard of work life, and they make their developers accountable for the quality of their own work, not the testers.

> *Reflective exercise: where has lack of quality had a serious cost – safety, financial, delays or customer satisfaction – in your working environment?*

2.2 Creating business justification for rebalancing focus on quality

Chapter 1 argued that getting things right could reduce delays and cost over-runs. However, there is a gulf between **the project manager** understanding that good project quality management will save time and money, and convincing **those authorising the budget** that they should invest in project quality. The following suggests approaches to justifying quality that can be useful in discussions with project boards.

2.2.1 The need to see past fire-fighting

For decades, cost-cutting has seemed like an end in itself, with the result that organisations are frequently short of resource. Those who **can't** or **won't** plan are given the perfect excuse; they are too busy dealing with today's problems to prevent tomorrow's.

Fire-fighters can become heroes, being rewarded for dealing with problems – the question 'Why was there a fire to put out in the first place?' is often ignored.

Fire-fighting today's problems is a huge drain on the organisation. It:

- Consumes huge amounts of effort that is WASTE – this effort is only needed because something has gone wrong and has to be put right.
- Consumes money that is WASTE – it is expensive to drag resource into fire-fighting as the project incurs delay costs or resource back-fill costs.
- Spends money INEFFICIENTLY – if you need something today, you pay a premium for it, and it may not be what you really need in the long term
- Distracts attention away from prevention of problems, so undermining quality attitudes.

The first step in justifying quality is to be clear that fire-fighting is EXPENSIVE. We need to see past the smokescreen and put fire prevention measures in place, this means planning for project quality.

2.2.2 The only cost you can cut without damaging the business is waste

Cutting in-house staff, facilities, contingency reserves and 'expensive' suppliers often has harmful side effects, as cutting resources also gets rid of capability and capacity to deliver benefit. Table 2.1 indicates, for each of these, the possible issues and likely risks of cost-cutting.

Reducing waste has no significant detrimental effects on the business.

TABLE 2.1 Project issues and risks from cost-cutting

Cost-cutting Focus	Issues may include	Risks include
In-house staff	Loss of knowledge and experience. Loss of specialist expertise. Loss of morale. Loss of thinking time.	Loss of culture. External staff are less controllable and consistent. Raised levels of problems and delays while fixing problems.
In-house facilities and contingency reserves	Loss of capability/capacity. Loss of resilience.	Dependence on external facilities. Much slower response to issues.
"Expensive" suppliers	Changing suppliers results in delays for knowledge-transfer and set-up. Loss of experience.	Knowledge transfer may be inadequate. "Cheap" suppliers may deliver substandard products.

28 Why manage quality?

The biggest waste in a project is often the fire-fighting required to put right quality issues, the result of making mistakes. Eliminating the waste of fire-fighting can remove a substantial cost to the project.

'More haste, less speed' is true. It takes time to recover from mistakes from over-hasty delivery. Getting things right saves life, time and money; getting things right results from effective quality management.

2.2.3 Constructing the case for project quality

The challenge for justifying quality spending is that its benefits are predominantly cost avoidance (reduced PONC, i.e. the total financial impact on the project of all consequences of quality failures). These savings are **potential** and **uncertain**, as failure costs are **predicted** with **estimated** probabilities and costs. After all, if the project is lucky, the quality issues may never arise, and actual failure cost if they do happen will only be known afterwards with certainty.

In contrast, Cost of Implementing Quality (CoIQ) is a **certain** cost, as it is calculated from the additional resource required, the time taken to plan, and the premium paid to suppliers.

This trade-off between certain costs and uncertain benefits is handled with statistical rigour in the actuarial calculation of insurance premiums, and by professional gamblers, where there is extensive data to analyse, but in projects, there is often not enough data to support a robust statistical analysis, leaving decisions to be made more subjectively.

Getting management support for improving quality is rarely easy, unless the consequences of failure are so catastrophic that even with tiny probabilities, quality still wins out – nuclear projects fall into this category, for instance. Figure 2.3 illustrates how increased investment in quality is more than compensated for by reduction in the cost of quality failures, the modest cost investment in quality assurance results in a much larger drop in the cost of rework and delays, while many costs are unaffected.

The following steps outline a sound process for justifying the investment in quality of both effort and funding.

Step 1: understand the approval process

It is essential to understand how your organisation appraises investment as approaches vary substantially. In some cases, cost avoidance is excluded from financial treatment of investment, so the quality benefits must be 'rebadged' in an acceptable way.

Step 2: identify a champion

A champion is a senior person in the organisation with both the influence and the motivation to support and push forward your quality proposal.

Why manage quality? 29

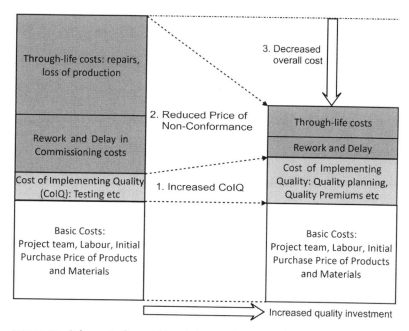

FIGURE 2.3 Schematic financial breakdown of improved quality within the project

Step 3: define and quantify business benefits

The business case must justify the investment planned, which requires defining the tangible benefits from quality improvements and estimating a robust financial value for them, as well as a realistic cost estimate. This requires research – itself needing time and resource.

Step 4: win support of stakeholders

Individual conversations with stakeholders help to get the commitment needed for quality investment through a shared understanding of the potential benefits.

Step 5: justify the business case with hard data

Collate the cost/benefit analysis by establishing:

- Project costs for achieving quality.
- Estimated price of non-conformance for the project, with and without effective quality management.

This requires quantifying quality failure scenarios, estimating the cost of quality to prevent those scenarios occurring, the PONC if they happen and probability of failure. The difficult parameter to estimate **defensibly** is the probability of a quality failure occurring.

Why manage quality?

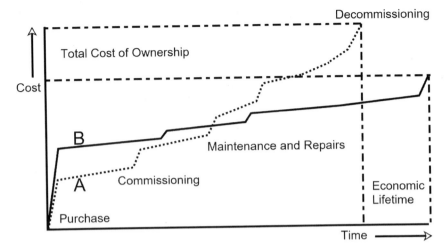

FIGURE 2.4 Contrasting the initial purchase price with total cost of ownership

It is important to consider the total cost of ownership (TCO) and economic lifetime in setting procurement targets. A low initial purchase price may be false economy – the scenario in Figure 2.4 illustrates how a low initial purchase price is more than wiped out by additional commissioning costs and through-life costs, leading to earlier decommissioning.

In Figure 2.4, Line A (dotted line) has a lower initial cost but with maintenance and repairs the total cost of ownership is higher. Line B has a higher initial cost but needs less maintenance. B has a longer economic lifetime and lower cost of ownership. Most people would choose option B if given all the information. Again, this leads to quality in the business case.

Step 6: create your business case presentation

A convincing business case requires convincing delivery of the information needed to convince others about the investment.

2.3 Conclusions of chapter

This chapter concludes that producing deliverables that are fit for purpose and conform to requirements:

1. Enhances safety.
2. Reduces delays.
3. Controls costs.
4. Enhances customer satisfaction.
5. Increases commercial success.
6. Increases project morale.

These are all factors in finding the optimal balance between managing cost, time and quality.

Waste is the only cost that can be cut without adverse consequences, and poor quality products are waste, as is the effort to deal with them.

Investment in improving quality across portfolio, programme or large project can be justified through a conventional financial approach. The investment of time and effort to estimate the cost and probability of quality failure is repaid through reduced price of non-conformance.

2.4 Bibliography

ATSB (2010) – http://www.atsb.gov.au/publications/investigation_reports/2010/aair/ao-2010-089.aspx

BEA (online) – https://www.bea.aero/uploads/tx_elydbrapports/f-sc000725a.pdf

Dale, B.G., Bamford, D. and van der Wiele T. (2016) 'Managing Quality: An Essential Guide and Resource Gateway', 6th edition, Wiley, ISBN: 9781119130932

Dale, B. G., van der Wiele T. van Iwaarden J. (2007) 'Managing Quality', 5th edition, Wiley, ISBN: 9781118762172

Hendricks, K. B. and Singhal V. R. (1996) 'Quality Awards and the market value of the firm: an empirical investigation', Management Sciences, 42(2), 415–436

Hutchens, S. (1989) 'What customers want: Results of ASQ/Gallup Survey', Quality Progress, February 1989, 33–36

ICE online – https://www.ice.org.uk/knowledge-and-resources/case-studies/design-and-construction-of-rion-antirion-bridge

NASA (2003) – https://www.nasa.gov/columbia/home/CAIB_Vol1.html

PRINCE2 (2009), 'Managing Successful Projects with PRINCE2®' 2009 edition, Axelos Ltd, ISBN: 9780113310593

Ryan, J. (1988) 'Consumers see little change in product quality', Quality Progress, December 1988, 16–20

Sargeant, A., Hudson, J. and Wilson, S. (2012) 'Donor complaints about fundraising: What are they and why should we care?' Voluntas, 23(3), 791–807

Young, R.R. (2003) 'The Requirements Engineering Handbook', Artech House, Boston. London, ISBN: 9781580532662

Further reading

Buttrick, R. (2005) 'The Project Workout', 3rd edn, FT Prentice Hall, London, ISBN: 0273681818

Morris, P. W. G. and Jamieson, H. A. (2004) 'Translating Corporate Strategy into Project Strategy', Project Management Institute, Newton Square, PA, ISBN: 1930699379

Columbia Disaster – http://www.youtube.com/watch?v=6R4ctaCBapM

3
WHO IS RESPONSIBLE FOR QUALITY?

It is **people** that make things happen in projects; processes, disciplines and tools just help.

As quality is critical to project success, it is the project, programme and portfolio managers who are accountable for it (although responsibility may be delegated). Striking the right balance between quality, cost and schedule by these leaders is vital for a successful outcome.

This chapter covers the quality roles and responsibilities of everyone on the project and its supply chain, and how introducing a quality culture helps.

It considers the challenges faced in changing entrenched attitudes and behaviours, and how to build acceptance of quality working.

It covers the value and use of third parties in quality assurance and control.

Learning outcomes for the chapter

After reading this, the reader should understand:

- Everyone is responsible for quality.
- Which project roles have which particular responsibilities for quality.
- Opportunities exist to involve third parties in ensuring supply chain quality.

3.1 Everyone is responsible for quality

Western culture's valuing of specialisation seems ever-increasing. The combination of a litigious 'it's not my fault, someone else should pay' culture, and top-down management putting people in ever-narrower roles means motivations for individuals to think about the 'big picture' are declining.

Quality thinking, like systems thinking, requires looking at that big picture, not just focusing on one element of it. Fitness for purpose and meeting requirements result from everyone thinking and working together; it is not possible for a small team of quality specialists, working on their own, to ensure quality products and outcomes are delivered.

Quality specialists are there to establish a quality culture and quality management system (QMS, the roles, responsibilities, processes and standards for ensuring quality results). This affects the way everyone within the organisation thinks and works, and provides the tools, methods and disciplines that enable everyone to work together towards a quality outcome. It is not the quality specialists who deliver quality; **it is the project team**, working in a quality-orientated way.

- **Key learning point – everyone is responsible for quality**

A successful project gets everyone working together, aiming for quality outcomes and using quality approaches and tools. This requires a quality culture within the project team – if the project team members don't follow best practice, how can anyone else be expected to?

3.2 Quality culture forms the foundation

Until fairly recently, business change was something that happened occasionally, and at the end of a change period everyone could breathe a sigh of relief and relax into a period of stability. That is no longer the case – business change has become continuous, and disruptive business changes are ever-more common. This need for constant change needs to be reflected in the organisation's culture.

Instilling a quality culture needs a drive from the top, with clear leadership from top management. Growing that culture depends very much on winning the hearts and minds of everyone in the organisation. Fostering that growth needs to be done by management at all levels, particularly supervisors and middle managers.

A culture change of this scale requires changes in attitudes, values and behaviour, achieved through a combination of leadership, training and education delivered to everyone down to the grass roots of the organisation and supply chain.

The aim is to create a working environment in which (adapted from Dale et al 2007):

- People work together in teams as the norm, and teams work collaboratively with other teams.
- Organisational silos are broken down, and effective dialogue occurs whenever relevant.
- People feel ownership of the outcomes they are working towards, aiming to delight customers, internal or external.
- Genuine mistakes are shared immediately without fear of punishment i.e. a 'no blame' culture.

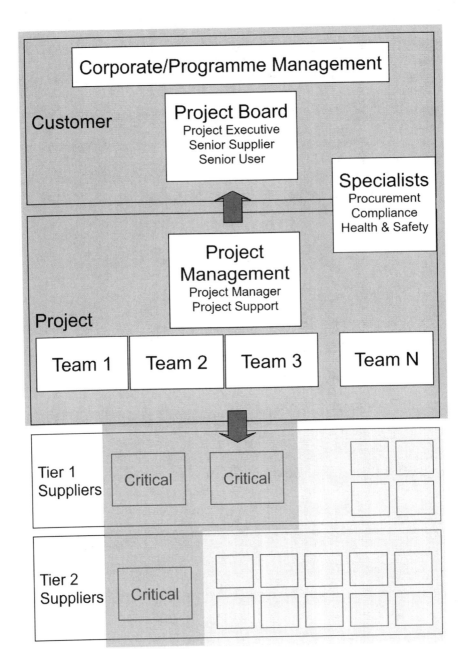

FIGURE 3.1 The scope of project team working

Who is responsible for quality? **35**

- Permanent solutions to problems are sought, from everyone, not just 'papering over the cracks'.
- The value of quality activities is recognised.

Empowering a team results in empowering individuals in the team, allowing them to be involved at all stages of quality management, not just those stages that directly affect them. This transition can be difficult for organisations, as it may force managers to consider their own role and value within the organisation.

> *Reflective exercise: why is working together towards a shared objective more productive? If you have experienced both 'blame cultures' and supportive cultures, which worked better, and why?*

Team working is a core enabler of successful quality management, so it cannot be restricted to within the company or organisation. The team may well include some or all of the supply chain; it should include representatives from end users through to component suppliers working together towards a joint vision of success: Case study 5 illustrates this. In this case, field engineers and the procurement department needed to work together to drive up quality in the supply chain.

Figure 3.1 shows a typical project structure with a project manager reporting to a project board. Various teams report to the project manager and each team has suppliers. Tier 1 suppliers provide goods and services to the project team using deliverables from tier 2 suppliers. Project success demands that requirements are communicated accurately through the supply chain, from the project team to the tier 1 and tier 2 suppliers and so on.

Where products of the supply chain are critical to project success, then their suppliers should be included in the project team no matter what supply chain tier they are in. Critical products (products critical to the success of the project) may include items such as bespoke products specific to the project, or products with more demanding performance and acceptance criteria than standard.

Extending teamworking across commercial and contractual boundaries facilitates smoother collaboration based on greater understanding and trust, aiming for shared objectives.

See Figure 3.1 and Case study 5 about extending team working across organisation boundaries.

CASE STUDY 5: ICL PERIPHERALS – TEAM WORKING IN THE SUPPLY CHAIN

In the 1980s, ICL, then the UK's premier computer supplier, recognised the need to focus its manufacturing activities where they delivered a competitive advantage and looked to procure those items they couldn't produce economically. The procurement team in ICL's manufacturing and logistics division had the job of selecting and buying-in peripheral devices such as printers, terminals and disk drives.

They were quietly passionate about the reliability of the devices they delivered to ICL's customers, and adopted the view that whatever the supplier claimed about the reliability of the product, it was the performance of the product in service that mattered. To assess this, they surveyed the field service engineers' reports.

The field service engineers worked for ICL UK, a different part of the company entirely. This made it very hard for the procurement team to interact directly with the engineers, so instead they 'mined' the data from engineers' report database. Analysing this allowed a lot of useful information about reliability to be fed back into the procurement process, with unreliable equipment receiving no further orders and the best-performing equipment being acquired instead.

The engineers were unaware of the use to which their database was being put, so the accuracy of the data logged was very variable – only half of the data records were usable by procurement, so a lot of useful information was being lost.

Procurement wanted a 'big data' solution, requesting a solution that automatically mined the existing data, to extract more useful information. However, achieving a solution required getting better quality data logged by the field service engineers. The outcome of the consultation on the project was not intelligent automation of the database analysis but a programme of communication to the field service engineers, explaining what data was required and why. In this way, collaboration and good communication were used in solving the problem rather than artificial intelligence.

3.3 Quality responsibilities within organisations

Introducing an effective scheme of quality management into an organisation requires engagement at all organisational levels:

- Executive and senior management.
- Middle management.
- Supervisors.
- Staff.

Reflective exercise: consider your organisation – what is the attitude of each of the groups above to changing the way you work? Is there enthusiasm for improvement, or 'change fatigue'?

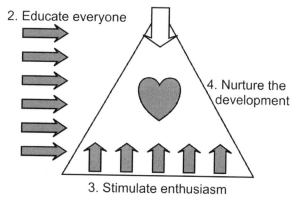

FIGURE 3.2 The main steps in introducing a corporate culture change

It is not easy to transform the organisation's culture into one in which everyone is committed to improving quality. Under pressure, people can revert to reactive ways of working and fire-fighting. This causes any quality initiative to break down. Although short-term fire-fighting may be unavoidable, strong proactive re-imposition of quality approaches is essential at the earliest opportunity. Figure 3.2 shows the main steps in introducing a corporate culture change.

3.3.1 Quality responsibilities of senior management and leaders

In any organisation with a top-down management ethos, the senior management team has to lead any quality initiative (Taylor and Wright, 2003):

- Formulating strategy.
- Creating and fostering a supportive atmosphere.
- Demonstrating the right values.

In co-operative organisations, where principles that are more democratic are applied, these activities must be done collaboratively.

As the quality management initiative progresses, senior managers must feed the commitment and confidence of all involved. They must:

- Put appropriate measures of quality in place and create realistic quality objectives.
- Avoid disillusionment with quality management.
- Handle any resistance towards a quality management approach.

This includes dealing with 'initiative fatigue', staff disillusioned after previous initiatives that were launched but management commitment to them died out.

38 Who is responsible for quality?

Positive actions in creating a project quality culture include:

- Explicitly handing quality responsibilities to members of the project team.
- Identifying quality risks and ensuring they are managed effectively.
- Including specific quality planning, assurance and control activities in the project plan.
- Defining the quantifiable measures of quality to be used.
- Communicate, communicate, and communicate! Make quality a regular feature of review and communicate about ways to continually improve.

and if possible:

- Planning and running quality training courses.
- Implementing and monitoring quality improvement plans with individuals.
- Facilitating regular quality self-assessment in a constructive way, avoiding blame.

3.3.2 Quality responsibilities of middle managers and team managers

Middle managers need to be committed to the concept of quality management. If the career of a manager has been founded on fire-fighting, this could easily be a problem. A lot of reassurance is required in these instances and very careful guidance and coaching needed to gain their commitment. Key elements of a middle manager's role in quality management include (adapted from Dale et al, 2007):

- Championing quality management to their team.
- Acting as a quality coach and mentor to their team.
- Making sure everyone has received adequate training.
- Protecting quality activities from criticism, dilution and threat.

3.3.3 Quality responsibilities of supervisors, staff and tier 1 suppliers

Supervisors and their staff are at the coalface of quality management and represent the largest stakeholder group. If these people are **not** committed to quality, there is little hope of success. Supervisors are directly responsible for:

- Acting as a quality coach and mentor to their team.
- Providing training on the quality techniques required.
- Running quality processes and ensuring their team to do the same.
- Checking that all relevant Standard Operating Procedures are available and used.
- Ensuring that all required quality data is collected accurately and logged.

- Ensuring that any quality issues are addressed, either first-hand or by escalation.
- Identifying, with their team, opportunities for improvement in quality.
- Reporting on the ease of use and effectiveness of the quality approach used.

3.4 Quality-related roles within projects

PRINCE2 recommends creating a common understanding of what the project will deliver and how it will be assessed. Without common understanding, acceptance disputes, rework, late changes and customer dissatisfaction could damage project success, even cause failure.

The roles and responsibilities in project quality management (shown in Table 3.1) have been adapted from the roles in the PRINCE2 (2007) standard.

For large projects, there are obvious key roles that are missing from Table 3.1. These specialist roles are not standard across all types of projects, and are shown in Table 3.2.

3.4.1 Quality responsibilities and the supply chain

Most major projects use sub-contracting extensively, so Chapter 7 covers managing Supply Chain quality in depth. We provide a brief overview of responsibilities here. Quality issues can start during anywhere in the supply chain including:

- Design.
- Raw materials.
- Manufacture.
- Testing.
- Transportation.

With the trend towards outsourcing, it is feasible that everything could be procured external to the project/organisation, and products are likely to have an extensive supply chain, possibly spanning the world. So, project quality management **must** extend beyond the project's organisation into the suppliers', as detailed in Table 3.3.

3.4.2 Building acceptance of quality management

Quality management initiatives, like so many other management initiatives, can attract adverse reaction for many reasons, including:

- Denial of the need for change.
- Conflict with existing demands.

40 Who is responsible for quality?

- Apathy – 'Seen it all before'.
- Disgruntlement with management style – imposition, not engagement.
- Seen as critical of the way the job is being done currently.
- Fear of the unknown, of being 'found out' as inadequate in the revised role.

TABLE 3.1 Roles and responsibilities in project quality management (adapted from PRINCE2)

Role	Responsibilities
Higher management Project Sponsor	Provide Quality Management System (QMS). Approve the overall project requirements and acceptance criteria.
	Agree how the QMS will be used.
	Accept the project on completion.
End user representatives	Provide functional requirements, quality and acceptance criteria.
	Provide non-functional requirements, including usability and performance minima.
	Facilitate effective management of requirements emergence in complex projects.
	Provide the people needed for user quality activities.
	Accept the solution delivered.
Supplier representatives, internal and external	Agree the QMS.
	Approve the quality planning, including contractors' plans etc.
	Provide resources for supplier quality activities.
	Check compliance with quality plans.
	Managing requirements emergence in complex projects.
Project Manager	Elicit and document the project's overall requirements.
	Elicit, document and maintain the detailed requirements.
	Liaise with external suppliers.
	Coach quality behaviours in the project team.
	Ensure that planned quality measures are being implemented.
	Manage requirements emergence in complex projects.
Team Managers (may be external) – responsible for delivering products for the project	Produce products compliant with requirements.
	Manage planned quality activities and report status regularly.
	Escalate to PM any risks to quality at earliest opportunity.
	Create quality records.
Project Support (Project or Programme Management Office) – includes Quality team	Provide administrative support for quality management.
	Compile the quality records.

Who is responsible for quality? **41**

TABLE 3.2 Additional quality-related roles and responsibilities in large projects

Role	Responsibilities
Compliance	Review all products' quality criteria and ensure that they make explicit any requirements for compliance with: • Legislation applicable at the project's base location • Local law (all locations involved outside the base jurisdiction) • Regulators' requirements
Health and Safety	Review all products' quality criteria and ensure that they make explicit any requirements for compliance with Health and Safety policy and relevant legislation.
Procurement	Review prospective suppliers and determined whether they are realistically capable of meeting, and likely to meet, the quality requirements. Negotiate with suppliers a contractual basis for the provision of products or services that are fully compliant with the quality requirements without jeopardising cost and time constraints. Negotiate with suppliers an agreed quality management strategy for their contract that is consistent with the project's. The project's quality management strategy integrates the customer's and suppliers' quality management systems.
External Suppliers	Approve and agree the product descriptions for those products they will be contracted to deliver. These will include the quality requirements and acceptance criteria. Agree a quality management strategy for the delivery of quality products that is consistent with the project's Define the quality plans to be used. Provide resources to undertake their quality responsibilities.
Systems Engineers/ Solution Architects/ Business Analysts	Ensure the scope of the project and solution have been explored comprehensively. Ensure the requirements are comprehensive. Ensure that human factors and interactions have been covered in the solution design.

Those resistant to the initiative may be middle managers or supervisors who claim that their time would be better spent elsewhere, not developing quality. It is important to stop adverse reactions quickly, because they spread quickly. It is important to engage the enthusiasm of the person, countering the adverse reaction and 'converting' them; people who are initially against an idea, once converted, can become the strongest protagonists.

It is common for people to respond well to being given responsibility. This can take the form of leading a quality activity. If some do not respond, their redeployment will become necessary to ensure a quality focus.

42 Who is responsible for quality?

TABLE 3.3 Additional quality roles and responsibilities in project supply chains

Project team responsibilities	• Clearly specify quality standards, tolerances and acceptance criteria, avoiding over-specification. • Operate rigorous change control with the customer. • Operate rigorous change control with the supplier. • If quality issues arise, strike a reasonable balance between time, cost and quality compromises. • Create and foster a "no blame" team spirit that allows suppliers to be open and honest about risks and issues with quality delivery; reward openness, discourage concealment by the supplier. • Insist on clearly testable interim milestones, with quality criteria, for progress tracking. • Insist on accurate and timely reporting of risks and issues relating to quality. • Foster a quality culture in the tier 1 suppliers. • Engage directly with suppliers below tier 1 if their products are on the critical path and have significant risk associated with them.
Procurement team responsibilities	• Check prospective suppliers; are they qualified and likely to meet the quality requirements? • Negotiate a contractual basis for products or services that are fully compliant with the quality requirements, without jeopardising cost and time constraints. • Negotiate with suppliers an agreed quality management strategy that is consistent with the project's. • Carry out supply chain vendor audits. • Negotiate the means of achieving synergies between supplier quality assurance (QA) and project QA activities. • Select and engage any third party inspection authorities required.
Suppliers' responsibilities	• Understand what makes the product(s) fit for purpose – query any possible misunderstanding (e.g. Technical Queries). • Deliver products that are fit for purpose. • Produce an agreed plan for achieving the quality requirements. • Operate rigorous change control with their customer (the project in the case of tier 1 suppliers). • Operate rigorous change control with their suppliers. • Report risks and issues relating to quality straight-away to manage expectations and build trust. • Co-operate fully with any third-party inspections authority appointed by their customer. • Apply responsibilities listed above under "project team" to their own suppliers. • Deliver products that meet the requirements and acceptance criteria specified.

The Channel Tunnel (Case study 6) explores the breakdown in project progress due to disintegration of working relationships and a focus on cost rather than outcomes.

Who is responsible for quality? **43**

CASE STUDY 6: CONFLICT IN THE SUPPLY CHAIN – THE CHANNEL TUNNEL

The Channel Tunnel project saw the relationship between supplier and customer break down, and resulted in work stopping. This resulted from a lack of consensus between supplier and customer regarding the risk and reward of delivering a quality solution, and a focus on cost rather than quality outcomes that even the banks regarded as wrong.

In 1986, Transmanche Link (TML) signed a contract with Eurotunnel – the owner and operator, to design and build the tunnel. At completion, there was an 80 per cent cost overrun. Part of the cost increase undoubtedly resulted from increased safety, security, and environmental requirements – a quality issue. The contract was unclear over who should bear the cost increases and why – arguably another quality issue.

Relationship problems between TML and Eurotunnel began to emerge quickly. Eurotunnel management wanted to demonstrate firmness towards TML as the original contract was let without competitive tendering, and Eurotunnel saw this as favouring TML. TML thought the contract fairly reflected the risks they were carrying.

Budget over-runs in 1988 triggered serious friction, and Eurotunnel leadership started to publicly criticise TML for its management of the project. This snow-balled with a series of press leaks, coming to a head in 1990 and threatening the whole project. Eurotunnel wanted TML to absorb the cost overruns; TML defended the original estimates, arguing that cost increases resulted from changes.

TML rejected a pro-Eurotunnel arbitration judgement, and successfully sued Eurotunnel for unpaid stage payments, but Eurotunnel's banks prevented payment until the dispute between the parties was settled. The banks persuaded Eurotunnel to compromise, and an agreement was finally reached 'hours before the receivers would have needed to be called in'. With a new attitude (and new management in place on both sides), project performance improved quickly.

An unreasonable focus on cost to the detriment of meeting requirements led to poor supplier management, a major breakdown in team-working between customer and supplier, and almost to the brink of disaster. Re-imposition of **reasonable** working recovered the situation.

Compiled from *The Independent* (1993, 1995) and several other sources.

3.4.3 Quality and the project team

The term 'team' tends to be used indiscriminately about people working together, but John Nicholson (1982) makes a distinction between people who work in a **group**, and those people working in a **team**, as compared in Table 9.3.

44 Who is responsible for quality?

TABLE 3.4 Group working versus team working (adapted from Nicholson 1982)

Characteristic	Behaviour IN GROUPS	Behaviour IN TEAMS
Working Together	Working independently.	Working interdependently.
Decision Making	Not involved in the decision-making process, leading to disenfranchisement.	The leader involves the team in decision-making to produce positive results.
Communication	Cautious about what they say, and game playing may occur. "Knowledge is power".	Open and honest communication is encouraged. People try to see the other's point of view.
Innovation	Suggestions are discouraged.	Suggestions are encouraged.
Disagreement	Seen as divisive and is not easily expressed.	Constructive and creative, open expression of opinions and feelings.
Conflict	Distrust. Conflicts are kept 'bottled up' which may lead to explosion.	Seen as an opportunity for new ideas and as a normal aspect of human interaction. The team works to resolve conflict quickly and constructively.
Commitment	People act like 'hired hands'.	People have a sense of ownership and are committed to the team and goals.
Priority	Conformance.	Performance.

The table emphasises that in a team there is open and honest communication, innovation is encouraged and there is open expression of opinions and constructive and creative approaches to resolving conflict. Such an environment is conducive to developing a 'sense of ownership' and working towards quality objectives. Approaches which foster team development and emphasise team members' contribution to quality are therefore encouraged. It should be noted that the 'team' may also include key suppliers and they need to be engaged and incentivised in finding solutions to ensure project quality.

3.5 External services and delegated inspection authorities

In can be appropriate to engage a third party in quality assessment. There is a wide range of suppliers offering services. These fall into two main categories:

- Specialist inspection authorities e.g. Lloyds Register, Bureau Veritas, TuV.
- Manufacturers offering inspection services as an adjunct to their own activities.

There are a whole set of reasons to use such services.

1 Regulatory or legal compliance

The requirement to engage third-party inspection authorities (TPIAs) is common where safety is a major issue e.g. in the nuclear industry, pressure vessels, food manufacturing and pharmaceuticals.

2 Technical capability

Use of a third-party inspection authority is a sensible option, possibly the only one, where the organisation does not have the in-house ability to do the inspection e.g. X-ray inspection of welds or forgings. The use of specialist test and inspection service suppliers ensures that the work will be carried out to high standards to give a high level of confidence.

3 Economic and commercial factors

Thorough inspection can be difficult, time consuming and expensive when carried out by project staff. The cost of engaging a third party may be lower because they are specialists in that field and already have all the equipment and skills to do the inspection. For instance, if a component is sourced from India or China, the use of a third-party inspection agency based near to the manufacturer could be significantly cheaper than flying an inspection team out.

During the project, issues around quality may strain the relationship between supplier and customer. This makes it vital to ensure that inspection results are indisputable by either party. Options to tackle this are limited:

- Joint testing by the customer and supplier.
- Testing by someone completely independent and trusted by both.

4 Language and cultural factors

George Bernard Shaw is quoted as saying 'England and America are two countries separated by the same language'; even with their shared heritage, language and the enormous cultural cross-fertilisation of television and films, misunderstandings still occur. An example of this is in describing an idea as 'interesting':

- To the Americans, this is positive and means the idea will be progressed.
- In England, this often means that the idea is **merely** interesting, and not worth progressing.

How much worse with countries that don't share either the same heritage or language? Local insights into language and culture safeguard the project against delays and errors due to misunderstandings.

46 Who is responsible for quality?

5 Project assurance

A third-party inspection authority can independently validate and verify the project's quality management to fulfil part of the project assurance function.

3.5.1 The value of specifications and standards

Specifications and standards are important in ensuring that the customer's requirements are understood when working with external inspection services and Delegated Inspection Authorities.

In every case, the project will still need to provide the specification of the component to be tested and the acceptance criteria, particularly the tolerances, and refer to relevant standards too.

3.6 Conclusions of chapter

The chapter shows that everyone on the project has quality responsibilities, and building a quality culture helps them meet their responsibilities.

There will always be pressures to focus on cost or time at the expense of quality, but these pressures can be resisted in a good quality culture – delivering a quality outcome is almost certain to be quicker and cheaper at the end of the project, delivering the best balance between time, cost and quality, and avoiding waste.

There is a substantial difference between people working independently as part of a 'group', and people working closely together as a 'team'. Teams work more efficiently and effectively than groups, so team working and team spirit boost project performance.

The responsibilities of the project extend down its supply chain, and team working over commercial and organisation boundaries helps greatly.

Changing entrenched attitudes and behaviours to build acceptance of quality working requires sustained management effort, and may result in some staff being deployed out of the project.

Third-parties can have an important and valuable role in quality assurance and control for a wide range of reasons.

3.7 Bibliography

Dale, B. G., van der Wiele, T., van Iwaarden J. (2007) 'Managing Quality', 5th edition, Wiley, ISBN: 9781118762172

PRINCE2 (2009) 'Managing Successful Projects with PRINCE2®' 2009 edition, Axelos Ltd, ISBN: 9780113310593

Taylor, W.A. and Wright, G.H. (2003) 'The impact of senior managers' commitment on the success of TQM programmes: an empirical study' International Journal of Manpower 24(5), 535–51

The Independent (1993) – http://www.independent.co.uk/news/business/eurotunnel-re solves-row-with-tml-march-opening-date-set-as-bank-of-england-secretly-brokers-pounds-1487652.html

The Independent (1995) – http://www.independent.co.uk/news/business/contractors-hit-back-at-eurotunnel-1603281.html

4

WHEN DOES QUALITY NEED TO BE MANAGED?

This chapter explains that the scope of quality management thinking has expanded progressively from inspection to Total Quality Management (TQM), as understanding has grown of how early investment in quality pays back through waste reduction, delay avoidance and improved customer satisfaction.

It describes the key tools and techniques of project quality management, before stepping through the lifecycle, looking at when they are applied, and what they achieve. In particular, it describes using a central quality register to link everything together.

Quality is not an alternative to other management objectives. Whatever the business is trying to achieve, and however it is trying to achieve it, quality must be incorporated into it. Delivering fitness-for-purpose and meeting requirements is something needing to be thought about at all times throughout the life-cycle of the project, and planning for acceptance (so justifying stage payments) is a commercially vital concern.

As good planning helps good performance, quality planning starts right at the beginning of a project.

Despite the pressure that project, programme and portfolio managers are always under, to demonstrate progress and to be controlling costs from the start of the project, the quality ideal is getting everything set up right first.

Learning outcomes for the chapter

After reading this chapter, the reader should understand:

- How the scope of project quality management has expanded to drive out waste and reduce delays from rework.
- How quality starts at the beginning of the project – fail to plan, plan to fail.

- What a quality management system (QMS) is, and its objectives.

4.1 The evolving scope of quality management

The oldest quality method, inspection, occurs late in the project lifecycle; as quality thinking progressed, quality activities have started earlier and earlier. TQM starts quality involvement at project inception and expands the breadth of quality thinking from products-only to management processes, as shown in Figure 4.1.

The figure uses manufacturing terms, as this is where it came from, but in the project context, these terms take on a wider meaning:

- Component – a product within the project's scope.
- Manufacturing process – the process or activity by which a product is created.
- Management process – a process that controls something else.
- People and culture – the human resources and their value system and behaviours.

4.1.1 Inspection

Inspection was the original method for ensuring quality. A sample or even all items would be tested against agreed criteria to see whether requirements had been met. There are a number of serious problems associated with inspection when used alone:

- The inspection process is time consuming and expensive in effort – the higher the confidence level required, the more time and cost involved.
- The cost of scrap or waste components found by inspection can be substantial.
- Inspection is after the event, there is no prevention component.

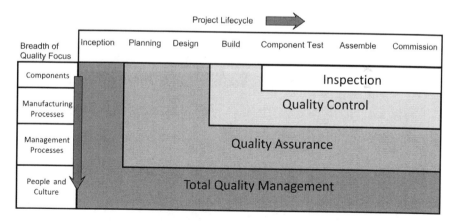

FIGURE 4.1 Advancing scope of quality thinking. Adapted from Dale et al (2007)

50 When does quality need to be managed?

- Inspection is typically the preserve of specialist inspectors, forming a potential bottleneck in production.

These problems drove the next phase of quality thinking, quality control.

4.1.2 Quality control

Quality control checks that quality requirements have been achieved. It is still based on inspection, but the thinking has increased in sophistication and scope. Rather than focusing purely on the components, products and assemblies i.e. the purely tangible outcomes, the focus expands to the processes that produce those outcomes. There are likely to be detailed specifications, formal quality procedures and appropriate paperwork. Quality control should be planned in an integrated way throughout the production process.

The focus of quality control remains on **detecting** cases where quality standards have not been met. This is still an expensive way of tackling quality and the risk of undetected quality issues reaching the end of process/supply chain is significant, as are the consequences.

'Prevention is better than cure' is the driver for the next step in thinking, quality assurance.

4.1.3 Quality assurance

Quality assurance is a proactive approach to quality being achieved, focusing on prevention rather than cure. This starts right at the design stage for each product. Most project management sources split the quality assurance ethos into two elements: **quality planning**, aiming to 'bake in quality', leaving the **quality assurance** function responsible for confirming that the quality plans are being followed.

The sorts of activities required to shift from cure to prevention include:

- Creating and applying a suitable Quality Management System that aims to deliver conformance to requirements (see Chapter 11).
- Quality planning from the start.
- Applying systems engineering disciplines to produce a design which is 'fit for purpose'.
- Designing each product/process to avoid defects.
- Training and motivating staff to avoid defects.

While:

- Using quality control tools.
- Gathering and analysing quality data.
- Improving (process) control.

Quality assurance still has its limitations, as it creates a quality ethos in production, without the same ethos in business leadership. This gap in thinking disappears in TQM.

4.1.4 Total Quality Management (TQM)

TQM builds further on quality assurance, extending quality management to all aspects of the organisation, its customers, its suppliers and its key business processes. TQM is a philosophy of continuously developing products, methods and processes ahead of competitors (Dale et al, 2016). Best practice in project quality management is consistent with TQM.

Eight quality management principles are defined in BS EN ISO 9000:2015 'Quality Management Systems. Fundamentals and Vocabulary':

1. Customer focus, on current and future needs, requirements, and expectations.
2. Leadership, achieving unity of purpose and direction.
3. Involvement of people at all levels.
4. Process approach to activities and resources.
5. Managing interrelated processes as a system.
6. Continuous improvement.
7. Decision-making based on analysing facts and hard data.
8. Mutually beneficial supplier relationships between an organisation and its suppliers.

Together, these principles define a culture of empowerment, respect, focus on achievement and good working relationships. The generation of conflict and need for fire-fighting are reduced, which should lead to a quieter life and more relaxed relationships. Nevertheless, this is not an easy transformation, as it is dependent on a consensus being achieved. The leaders need to lead in the new way; the followers need to respond appropriately.

A likely driver to motivate this change is reducing the cost associated with waste.

4.1.5 The Quality Management System

The Quality Management System (QMS) is a core concept in quality thinking, and is described by BS EN ISO 9000:2015 (BSI, 2015) as:

'Comprising [those] activities by which the organisation identifies its objectives and determines the processes and resources required to achieve desired results, and managing the interacting processes and resources required to provide value and realise results for relevant interested parties.'

It adds that a QMS helps optimise the use of resources, and identifying actions to provide satisfactory i.e. quality, products and services.

When does quality need to be managed?

A more concise definition is:

The set of roles (with associated responsibilities), disciplines, processes, and standards that define how the organisation targets and delivers quality products and services.

4.1.6 How investment in quality EARLIER in the project lifecycle reduces cost

Figure 4.2 illustrates how investment in quality earlier in the project lifecycle reduces total cost, by driving down the price of non-conformance while controlling the cost of implementing quality.

The stages in Figure 4.2 represent progress in an organisation's journey in implementing quality. The figure shows this divided into five stages:

Stage 1: The organisation incurs 'failure costs' as a result of poor quality of its products. Investment in detection earlier in the production process traps out-of-specification components before they are assembled. This means that as detection costs rise, the failure costs and total cost fall. The cost of detection is less than the price of non-conformance.

Stage 2: As quality problem detection costs rise through greater investment, the failure costs continue to fall. Investment in improving detection is of limited value, however, because it doesn't reduce the cost of scrappage. Investment in prevention allows a reduction in failure costs as problems are avoided. Detection costs can also be reduced and the total costs are lower as there are fewer quality problems.

Stage 3: Further investment in prevention allows detection costs to be reduced significantly. The effectiveness of prevention allows a drop in total cost much better than for detection alone.

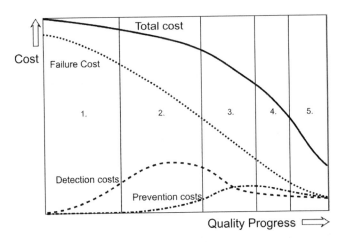

FIGURE 4.2 How investment in quality reduces cost – adapted from BSI (1990)

When does quality need to be managed? 53

Stage 4: Steadily improving quality management results in both prevention and inspection costs falling at the same time as the price of non-conformance falls too. This stage is heavily dependent on supplier quality management.

Stage 5: Continuous improvement, a virtuous circle, getting better and better. The failure costs are at a minimum, the prevention and detection costs are also low since problems have been resolved.

> *Reflective exercise: what techniques do you use to achieve quality in your life outside work?*

4.2 The toolkit supporting successful delivery during project initiation

Before looking at which quality management activities occur at each stage of the project, let's look at the principal tools to use.

The APM BoK (APM, 2012) states: 'Validation against overall requirements and verification against specifications and designs are both important. Verification ensures the deliverable is being built right; validation ensures that the right deliverable is being built'.

Validation is the process of confirming the completeness and correctness of requirements i.e. that the documented requirements are the true requirements and that we are building the right product.

Verification is the process of confirming that the designed and built product will fulfil the specification (i.e. that the solution is being built right).

The 'V Model' schematic view of the typical project lifecycle, shown in Figure 4.3, shows how customer engagement with suppliers varies with time – high

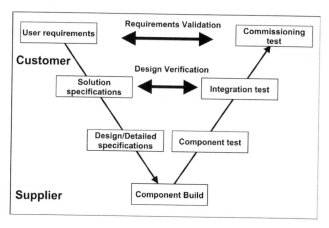

FIGURE 4.3 'V Model' schematic view of the typical project lifecycle

54 When does quality need to be managed?

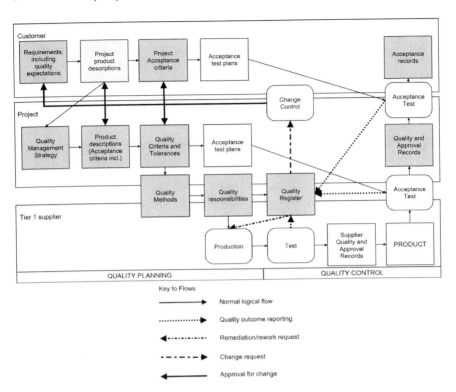

FIGURE 4.4 Quality flow diagram for the project lifecycle (adapted from PRINCE2 2009 Figure 6.1)

at start and finish, reduced in the middle. This makes using the tools requiring heavy input from the customer at the right time very important. Verification of the solution, and validation of the requirements, occur late in the project lifecycle, which can reveal fundamental flaws late. This is such a common problem in IT projects, it is discussed in Chapter 10.

Expanding on Figure 4.3, Figure 4.4 (which is consistent with PRINCE2) shows the quality flow for the whole project life cycle and shows how the quality management tools in the project toolkit fit together, with the information flows between them, to deliver quality outcomes.

In this chapter, we detail some key tools individually:

- Change control (and configuration/version management).
- Requirements and acceptance criteria.
- Project quality plan:
  - Roles and responsibilities.
  - Planning, tracking, reporting and recording of quality activities.
  - Standards and auditing to be applied.
  - Inspection, testing and review tools and techniques.
- Supplier quality plan:

When does quality need to be managed? **55**

- Roles and responsibilities.
- Planning, tracking, reporting and recording of quality activities.
- Standards and auditing to be applied.
- Inspection, testing and review tools and techniques.
- Contracts:
  - Commercial basis.
  - Scope and products to be provided.
  - Quality terms.

The next chapter (5) then covers tool usage during each stage of project execution.

4.2.1 Project change control and configuration (version) management

Problems within a project are often caused by different people working from different versions of information, especially engineering drawings. How to prevent this is simple and well-understood: implement rigorous project change control and configuration (including document version) management.

Configuration management is vital to avoiding mistakes and misunderstandings. It is a key component of managing quality within a project.

BSI (2017), BS ISO 10007:2017 'Quality management systems: Guidelines for configuration management' gives extensive guidance on this.

Most organisations will have a programme management office offering these services before the project even starts – if not, change and configuration management need setting up as the very first step.

4.2.2 Requirements and acceptance criteria

Right at the start of the project, it is important to be very clear what the project is trying to achieve. This is defined by two elements:

- What the project must deliver (in **business outcomes**, not just products).
- The acceptance criteria for the project as a whole.

Completion of most projects requires the delivery of many products, including documents, physical items and services. Each of these needs documented requirements and acceptance criteria.

The following points cover the key quality information required for each product:

1. **Purpose to be fulfilled** (to confirm 'fitness for purpose').
2. The products/deliverables/components/services that **together** will satisfy the requirements.

56 When does quality need to be managed?

3. What **quality criteria** must the product meet? How will quality be assessed, what **tolerances** are acceptable and **standards** must be satisfied? How do quality standards apply to the supply chain?
4. What **quality methods** need to be applied? Who will apply them?
5. **Acceptance criteria**.

Agreeing and documenting acceptance criteria early in the project helps to clarify any uncertainty about the project when there is still time to address it. Acceptance criteria can be flexed as the project develops, under change control.

As a project example, the Scottish Parliament building had an aspirational aim of being 'the visual embodiment of exciting constitutional change' (Cartlidge, 2003). This is subjective and cannot be tested – it is therefore unsuitable as a measure of success. Such criteria need to be converted or broken down into a set of criteria that are testable. Defining the acceptance methods and acceptance plan in parallel to the acceptance criteria themselves ensures that the criteria specified can actually be tested and confirmed.

Case study 7 illustrates the life-changing cost to a worker where requirements were not fully understood.

4.2.3 Project quality plan

Fail to plan, plan to fail! The APM BoK states: 'Quality planning involves the preparation of a quality management plan that describes the processes and metrics

---

CASE STUDY 7: INAPPROPRIATE MATERIAL SUPPLIED FOR A SAFETY-CRITICAL APPLICATION (PERSONAL COMMUNICATION)

During refurbishment of a power station, plywood was used as scaffolding walkway material in a high humidity environment. It had to safely bear the weight of workers using the walkway and not deteriorate in the environment. However, this requirement had not been translated into a minimum specification for the material. Plywood had been procured by **specifying** the Grade only, not by defining the purpose it was **required** for, nor the thickness. Communication errors resulted in plywood being supplied that was not fit for purpose (too thin, sensitive to moisture, resulting in it becoming too weak). The flooring failed, a worker fell through and was badly injured.

Reflective exercise: create the requirements, acceptance criteria and acceptance plan for your next major purchase.

that will be used. It needs to be agreed with relevant stakeholders to ensure that their expectations for quality are correctly identified.'

Quality planning starts in the early stages of a project, but its ramifications extend to the very end i.e. to project acceptance and shutdown (and ideally even further – operations, and even decommissioning).

The first important output of quality planning is the project quality plan (APM 2012). This document lays down the way that quality will be managed throughout the project to achieve the quality outcomes and objectives required, including:

- Roles and responsibilities.
- Planning, tracking, reporting and recording of quality activities.
- Standards and auditing to be applied.
- Inspection, testing and review tools and techniques.

Where multiple organisations are involved in projects – especially customer and supplier businesses – conflicts between multiple QMSs may occur. The project quality plan needs to define how all the QMSs, including those of customer and suppliers, will integrate and operate together within the project.

The project quality plan is not static – it needs to flex in response to changing situations within the project. This requires rigorous review and change control throughout the project, as any change to the quality plans ultimately links back to project success.

Although this is commonly a standalone document, the diversity of the information held is so wide that it may well be better to hold it in an electronic repository as a virtual document composed of extracts from other, more specialist, documents. This eases change management and version control.

4.2.4 Supplier's quality plan

The supplier needs to provide a quality plan for ensuring the quality of each of the products they are supplying. The nature of their quality plan is linked to the complexity and risk associated with the products.

At the very simplest end of the spectrum, the supply of non-safety-critical wood screws for use in an office environment would not require a distinct quality plan! At the spectrum's other end, the supplier's quality plan for a major component (replacement boiler, aircraft engine) can be as comprehensive as that for the entire project.

Agreeing the appropriate level of detail in the supplier's quality plan is a vital task in project quality management.

Quality is a major consideration in supplier selection. Requesting a draft quality plan as part of the tender process has the following advantages:

- Quality is explicitly included in supplier selection and risk assessment.
- The prospective supplier understands how the project operates.
- An otherwise viable supplier with poor quality management can be rejected.

4.2.5 Contracts and their part in delivering quality

Any agreement between two parties can be considered a contract, even if those parties work for the same organisation.

Contracts internal to an organisation are rarely treated formally and are normally covered by standard project documentation unless a service level agreement applies. Where the second party is a separate legal or commercial entity, a contract is put in place.

The contract is the legally binding definition of what products/services are to be supplied, and failure to adequately define quality requirements and acceptance criteria is likely to lead to misunderstandings, delays, cost escalation and potentially, conflict. The contract document itself does not need to contain all the quality requirements and acceptance criteria however it must refer to the documents that do. Such documents MUST be under rigorous change and version control to avoid dispute.

4.3 Tools used to deliver quality during project execution

Quality Control implements the quality activities, tests and results that have been planned, and logs the results, raising corrective actions as necessary. It involves:

- Completing the planned quality activities (e.g. quality inspections or testing).
- Logging results and approvals meticulously in the records specified.
- Managing any non-conformances discovered, and their rectification.
- Gaining and logging acceptance, from the person responsible.

It uses a number of different tools, including:

1. Quality register.
2. Test/inspection plan.
3. Quality methods, test and inspection techniques.
4. Test/inspection equipment.
5. Test/inspection log.
6. Corrective action request.
7. Supplier's quality plan.
8. Acceptance report.

4.3.1 Quality register – creating the 'big picture'

There are obvious benefits to the project if all the quality activities planned, and the results from those activities, are compiled into a single 'big picture' for the project. A clear record of all the quality management activities and results directly confirms the project's reports of progress. Keeping track of these is an administrative role usually fulfilled by the project office/project support team requiring the active support of **everyone**, using a repository, known by a variety of names, but we shall refer to it as the quality register.

The quality register contains all planned quality activities and milestones, and logs the results from all quality activities already undertaken (including reviews, inspections, interim testing, and acceptance decisions). It is set up while the products and acceptance criteria are being decided, early in the project. It is then maintained throughout the project, coupled tightly to the project plan as it changes/flexes. It must be meticulously configuration-managed/version controlled.

The scale and detail of the quality register needs to be tailored to the project's needs, and can vary considerably between projects. PRINCE2 offers guidance on this.

4.3.2 Test/inspection plan

How do you know if a deliverable is complete and fit for purpose? This is the purpose of the test plan. The detail and rigour of the testing and inspection planned needs to be risk-based, driven by the consequences of failure (not the purchase price). The greater the risk associated with the failure of the product, the more testing/inspection is required to achieve a satisfactory level of confidence.

4.3.3 Quality methods, test and inspection techniques

As a non-compliant component is built up into ever-larger assemblies and then the final product, so the cost of correcting any defects rises. It is easier to correct a design fault at the design document stage than during testing of the finished product (or, worse, in operational use). This means quality methods applied in the design process, early in the project, are potentially the most cost-effective.

'In-process' quality methods aim to build quality into the product. 'Appraisal' quality methods assess the products once finished. As correcting defects gets more expensive the longer they remain undetected, in-process methods offer the greater potential for cost saving.

4.3.4 Test/inspection equipment

Test and inspection equipment is specific to the testing and inspection needed. It ranges from Vernier gauges to software regression test tools. The test equipment should be specified during quality planning.

Once the equipment has been selected, due to sensitivity, precision, accuracy or other limitations on the test equipment or method, its selection has to be recorded and go under change control, to avoid substitute equipment being used that is not up to the job.

4.3.5 Test/inspection log

Adequate records provide confidence that a product has successfully passed all the tests and inspections it should have. Recording results from test/inspection needs

60 When does quality need to be managed?

to match the detail and rigour of the test plan. Accurate and detailed test logs are very beneficial afterwards when:

- Tracking down the cause of failures in service.
- Protecting the company against liability claims.
- Improving processes.

Where non-conformances are found, they must be logged and corrective action instigated. This may involve a stand-alone non-conformance register, or 'bug log' in the case of software development.

4.3.6 Corrective action request

This is a formal, documented request to the supplier to fix a non-conformance that has been found during testing or inspection. All corrective action requests must be tracked through to retest of the corrected product and its acceptance, or agreement to a 'concession' that the requirement need not be met.

4.3.7 Acceptance report

Acceptance reports are vital tools in quality management as they state clearly and unambiguously whether the product has met all the requirements and been accepted as fit for purpose.

After acceptance, the product moves into its warranty phase, and the supplier can expect payment of any stage payment associated with acceptance of the product. Acceptance must not be given lightly as after this point, the only changes possible to the product are:

- Repairs and rectification under the terms of the warranty.
- Modifications, almost certainly paid for, under the terms of the contract.

Acceptance reports must state precisely **what** has been accepted, **why** it has been accepted and **who** is doing the acceptance (referencing the appropriate quality plan, quality records and quality register respectively).

4.4 Conclusions of chapter

Early investment in planning for quality reduces waste, holding down costs and minimising expensive delays. Balancing early investment in quality against focusing on cost and schedule reduction is vital to avoid early apparent savings that later result in expensive delays and failures – project success is monitored throughout, but assessed **on completion**.

The development of quality thinking scope, from inspection through Quality Control and Quality Assurance to Total Quality Management, is explained.

This chapter concludes that projects should adopt a TQM approach to quality management, investing early in quality planning to ensure forecast benefits can and will be delivered.

It describes the key 'tools' of project quality management, explaining what they achieve. These are split into two groups, project initiation and project execution.

Tools and techniques associated with project initiation include:

- Project change and configuration (version) management.
- Requirements and acceptance criteria.
- Project quality plan.
- Supplier's quality plan.
- Contracts.

Tools and techniques associated with project execution:

- The quality register.
- Test and inspection plans.
- Quality methods, test and inspection techniques.
- Test and inspection log.
- Corrective action request.
- Acceptance report.

Using a central quality register to link all quality plans and records together gives a clear view of true project achievement so far.

4.5 Bibliography

BSI (2017) 'BS ISO 10007:2017 Quality management systems: Guidelines for configuration management', British Standards Institution, ISBN: 9780580942570

BSI (2015), 'BS EN ISO 9000:2015 Quality management systems, Fundamentals and Vocabulary', British Standards Institution, ISBN: 9780580788789

BSI (1990) 'BS 6143-2:1990 Guide to the economics of quality. Prevention, appraisal and failure model', British Standards Institution, ISBN: 0580187292

Cartlidge, D. (2003) 'Procurement of Built Assets', Routledge, ISBN: 9780750658195

Dale, B.G., van der Wiele T., van Iwaarden J. (2007) 'Managing Quality', 5th edition, Wiley, ISBN: 9781118762172

PRINCE2 (2009) 'Managing Successful Projects with PRINCE2®' 2009 edition, Axelos Ltd, ISBN: 9780113310593

Further reading – requirements

Alexander, I. and Stevens, R. (2002) 'Writing Better Requirements', Addison-Wesley, Boston

Robertson, S. and Robertson, J. (2004) 'Requirements-led Project Management: Discovering David's Slingshot', Addison-Wesley, Boston

5

QUALITY MANAGEMENT THROUGHOUT THE PROJECT LIFECYCLE

This chapter goes through the extended project lifecycle (APM 2012), stage by stage, recommending and explaining the project quality activities at each stage and their role in preventing costly errors.

Learning outcomes for the chapter

After reading this chapter, the reader should understand:

- At which stage in the project lifecycle each quality tool needs to be used.

The exact list of stages depends on the type of project. We have attempted to further detail the five-stage, high-level and generic models offered by APM, PMI and PRINCE2 to stages more meaningful to quality management in engineering projects. These more detailed stages are relevant to most projects:

1. Concept.
2. Definition.
3. Delivery.
   i. Requirements capture.
   ii. Planning.
   iii. Contracting.
   iv. Design.
   v. Build.
   vi. Acceptance.
   vii. Integration and Commissioning.
4. Hand-over – normally the end-point of the project.

Quality management throughout the project lifecycle **63**

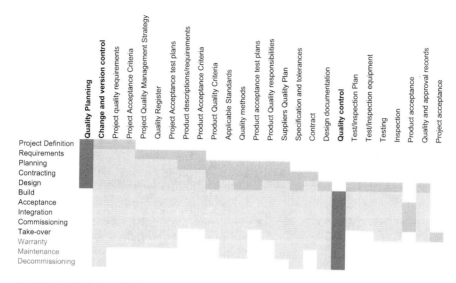

FIGURE 5.1 Relationship between quality tools and life-cycle stages

5. Benefits realisation.
   i. Warranty.
   ii. Operations and maintenance.
   iii. Decommissioning.

Figure 5.1 summarises when in the lifecycle a quality tool is created/identified (dark) and where it is used and maintained (pale).

We now go through the lifecycle stages, discussing these tools and techniques.

5.1 Concept stage

The concept stage creates the vision the project is trying to achieve. The key quality outcome here is an understanding of what success will look like in high-level terms.

5.2 Definition stage – getting the customer focus

Steve Jobs, Apple Founder *'You can't ask customers what they want and try to give that to them. By the time it's built, they'll want something new' (Inc. Magazine, 1989)*

The definition stage creates the roadmap of how the project will deliver the vision, defining the solution, the schedule and estimating the budget required.

Table 5.1 illustrates the quality documentation and tools used in this project phase.

Quality expectations can vary dramatically between applications – take pump durability:

64 Quality management throughout the project lifecycle

TABLE 5.1 Quality Outputs and Tools of Project Definition

Quality outputs	Quality tools used and maintained
• Project Change Control (mechanism) • Project Quality Requirements • Project Acceptance Criteria	

- The pump/turbine in a hydro-electric electricity-generating/pump storage scheme, for example Dinorwic in Wales, needs to last for decades with little maintenance while handling thousands of tonnes of water every day.
- The fuel pump in space rocket's motor only needs to last a few minutes.

The customer's top-level quality criteria should ideally convey the spirit of their requirements. Breaking these down into more detailed acceptance criteria will drive the solution. Any proposed solution must be assessed against those high-level criteria.

PRINCE2 explains that getting the project requirements and acceptance criteria reasonably correct at the start of the project helps create a shared understanding between all stakeholders, but especially the project team and the customer, of what success will look like. Scope can be controlled and scope creep avoided through a shared understanding of project objectives if the following are defined clearly and agreed:

- The project scope (what is to be addressed, what is to be excluded).
- The critical success criteria of the project (what it is aiming for).
- The products required and their quality criteria.
- The acceptance criteria for the project (including tolerances).
- Responsibilities for acceptance.

Meeting the requirements as defined doesn't guarantee success, however, as Case study 8 shows.

5.3 Delivery stage – turning ideas into reality

We have split the delivery stage, which is typically most of the project, into seven elements:

1. Requirements capture.
2. Planning.
3. Contracting.
4. Design.
5. Build.
6. Acceptance.
7. Integration and commissioning.

We now look at each of these in more detail.

Quality management throughout the project lifecycle **65**

CASE STUDY 8: THE MILLENNIUM DOME – TECHNICALLY A SUCCESS, COMMERCIALLY A FAILURE (NAO, 2000)

The Millennium Dome project, despite some setbacks, was functionally a success, delivering the experience desired and an iconic landmark. In 2000, it was the top tourist attraction in the UK and visitors were delighted.

Unfortunately, it didn't hit its commercial targets. The entire budget was based on a forecast of 12 million visitors; in reality, only 6.5 million arrived. The estimate of 12 million was based on the Empire Exhibition in Glasgow (1938) which achieved this in just six months, but was before mass television ownership or the Internet.

This project was criticised heavily by the media from early in its life, targeting the politicians behind the Dome.

One wonders if it might have been a commercial success if its image hadn't been tarnished so thoroughly before it even opened. Its failure was one of expectations, not execution.

5.3.1 Delivery stage: requirements capture

Once the project is defined, a project quality plan is prepared, defining how quality will be achieved and assessed, then the requirements need to be understood and documented.

The stakeholders' (and especially users') desires and needs are documented as requirements. Clear requirements and their acceptance criteria form the foundations for managing stakeholder expectations, and provide the basis for assessing project success.

Table 5.2 illustrates the quality documentation and tools used in this project phase.

Requirements include quality criteria and tolerances, which lead to defining the quality methods and responsibilities. Focusing requirements on outcomes relevant to the customer's business ('I want to improve ...'), rather than specifying in fine design detail how it will be achieved ('I want a database of...') gives the

TABLE 5.2 Quality Outputs and Tools of Requirements Capture

Quality outputs	Quality tools used and maintained
• Project Quality Plan/Quality Management Strategy	• Project Change Control
	• Project Quality Requirements
• Project Quality Register	• Project Acceptance Criteria
• Project Acceptance Test Plans	
• Product Descriptions/Requirements	
• Product Acceptance Criteria	

66 Quality management throughout the project lifecycle

experts designing the solution maximum scope to deliver the greatest benefit at the lowest cost.

Over-specification is a real threat to projects through:

- Creating delays through challenges in trying to meet the specification.
- Adding greatly to costs ('gold-plating').
- Excluding the expertise of the supplier in optimising the solution design.

Requirements capture often results in extensive documentation that is difficult to understand as a whole – this makes it hard to validate or verify. Commonly, especially with IT, only when the final project solution enters acceptance testing is it realised that it does **not** satisfy business needs. Requirements management is covered in more detail in Chapters 9 and 10.

Once the requirements are initially agreed, they go under change control. Quality criteria are an integral part of the requirements for each item. As soon as the first requirements are agreed, the project team needs to set up the Quality Register.

Poorly defined and untestable requirements can lead to huge problems, as the Scottish Parliament Building, Case study 9, indicates.

Requirements particularly important for major projects

There are some particular types of requirements that have a major impact on total cost of ownership. These are:

CASE STUDY 9: SCOTTISH PARLIAMENT BUILDING – CHANGING REQUIREMENTS

The Scottish Parliament building is a good example of a project where the politics of the situation combined with poor quality management to deliver late with massive cost overruns, although arguably meeting the objectives of the original vision.

From the start, the project created controversy. Many choices, including location and use of imported materials, were criticised by politicians and the media, resulting in a long stream of changes. The design evolved progressively as more stakeholders were involved. It opened over 3 years late. The final cost, estimated at £414 million dwarfed initial estimates of £10 million – £40 million (Cartlidge, 2003). However, the finished product has received numerous awards, including the 2005 Stirling Prize, and still attracts criticism in the media.

Reflective exercise: consider the Scottish Parliament building project – is it a failed or successful project?

Quality management throughout the project lifecycle   **67**

- Availability – the fraction of the time available for use.
- Durability – how long it should last without major refurbishment.
- Reliability – how often it is acceptable for the product to break down.
- Maintainability – how easily and economically it can be kept operational.
- Operability – the levels of training, user turn-over, and human errors acceptable.
- Adaptability – how easily it can be upgraded to meet future needs.

Addressing these requirements fully should result in a project outcome remaining fit for purpose during its planned life.

5.3.2 Delivery stage: planning

All project plans must include appropriate quality actions, particularly testing and inspection. Not allowing enough time to test is one common reason for project problems.

Table 5.3 illustrates the quality documentation and tools used in this project phase.

Planning needs to consider how the project will meet quality criteria, and allocate responsibilities, budgets and time provisions. It has to allow for necessary knowledge being obtained and incorporated into later stages of the project e.g. the results from a pilot are fed back into designing later stages of the project. Active risk management (see Chapter 9) helps drive the right quality effort at the right time.

Many major projects operate in a regulated environment where specific testing is mandatory. Early recognition of the need to involve third parties in testing is vital:

- The test organisation has to be selected.
- A price has to be negotiated.
- Their effort has to be built into the project schedule, and booked.
- Prerequisites for test have to be identified as dependencies, and planned for.

TABLE 5.3 Quality Outputs and Tools of Planning

Quality outputs	Quality tools used and maintained
• Refined Product Descriptions/ Requirements	• Project Change Control
	• Project Quality Requirements
• Refined Product Acceptance Criteria	• Project Acceptance Criteria
• Product Quality Criteria	• Project Quality Plan/Quality Management
• Applicable Standards applied to Products	Strategy
• Quality Methods defined	• Project Quality Register
• Product Acceptance Test Plans	• Project Acceptance Test Plans
• Product Quality Responsibilities agreed	• Product Descriptions/Requirements
• Draft prospective supplier quality plans	• Product Acceptance Criteria

5.3.3 Delivery stage: contracting

> *Reflective exercise: put yourself in the place of your suppliers – what do you need to know to deliver a solution that is fit for purpose, meeting all the requirements?*

Table 5.4 illustrates the quality documentation and tools used in this project phase.

Contracting is a communication phase: success for contracting **from a quality perspective** is that both parties have a shared understanding of what the supplier will deliver and that it will be fit for purpose. If commercial considerations are allowed to interfere with the effectiveness of this communication, it will reduce the chances of a successful outcome. The paradox is that the quality perspective requires working very closely, almost intimately, with the supplier, building an in-depth mutual understanding, but the commercial perspective drives negotiating the best price. Managing this paradox calls for excellent team working between the project and procurement teams:

- The project team needs to work closely with procurement staff to ensure they have the best possible quality information, ensuring they can order exactly what is needed.
- The procurement team needs to work closely with the project team to ensure that commercial optimisation doesn't have an adverse quality impact.

TABLE 5.4 Quality Outputs and Tools of Contracting

Quality outputs	Quality tools used and maintained	
• Standards to be applied to supplied Products	• Project Change Control	• Product Acceptance Criteria
• Quality Methods defined (supplier)	• Project Quality Requirements	• Product Quality Criteria
• Product Acceptance Plans	• Project Acceptance Criteria	• Applicable standards applied to products
• Product Quality Responsibilities agreed	• Project Quality Plan/ Quality Management Strategy	• Quality Methods defined
• Supplier quality plans	• Project Quality Register	• Product Quality Responsibilities agreed
• Refined Product Quality Criteria	• Project Acceptance Test Plans	• Draft prospective supplier quality plans
• Specifications and tolerances (supplier)	• Product Descriptions/ Requirements	
• Contract		

Quality management throughout the project lifecycle **69**

- The contract price needs to include a fair profit, and enough contingency to handle minor hiccups during the project, for the supplier – once the contingency is exhausted, change requests/variation notices will cause additional expenditure, and probably delays too.

5.3.4 Delivery stage: design

Design takes the project requirements and creates the specification for the solution (and its components) that will meet them.

Table 5.5 illustrates the quality elements created and tools used in this project phase.

Consulting stakeholders and end-users throughout the design process helps to maintain their ownership of the solution and aligns their expectations as the design takes shape. This helps the designers to create a solution that the stakeholders agree meets their requirements and acceptance criteria, as the best-fit within time and cost constraints.

Technical innovations in the solution can be considered, as they may offer a better solution, but they risk delays, cost overruns or blind alleys of development. Innovation is a risk to be managed carefully and proactively.

Powerful de-risking techniques include:

- Modelling and simulations.
- Concept demonstrators.
- Technology demonstrators.

TABLE 5.5 Quality Outputs and Tools of Design

Quality outputs	Quality tools used and maintained	
• Design Documentation	• Project Change Control	• Quality Methods defined
• Product Quality Criteria (for components)	• Project Quality Requirements	• Agreed Product Quality Responsibilities
• Quality Methods (for components)	• Project Acceptance Criteria	• Refined Standards applied to supplied Products
• Product Acceptance Test Plans (for components)	• Project Quality Plan/Quality Management Strategy	• Quality Methods defined (supplier)
• Specifications and tolerances (in-house)	• Project Quality Register	• Product Acceptance Test Plans
• Test/Inspection Plans	• Project Acceptance Test Plans	• Supplier quality plans
• Test/Inspection Equipment (specified)	• Product Descriptions/ Requirements	• Refined Product Quality Criteria
• Design verification against requirements	• Product Acceptance Criteria	• Specifications and tolerances (supplier)
• Quality records	• Product Quality Criteria	• Contract
• Change Requests	• Standards applied to Products	

70 Quality management throughout the project lifecycle

- Pilot implementations.
- Phased deployments.
- Value Engineering ('Achieving Excellence in Construction', web archive).
- 'Red Team' reviews, where experts outside the project critically appraise all assumptions, plans and implications.

All of these techniques have substantial collateral value in helping to validate the requirements early in the project. Systematic evaluation against the requirements as the design is developed ensures on-going verification of the project output's design meeting those requirements.

Verification of the design's fitness for purpose more commonly completes late in the project, as the Teton Dam, Case study 10, demonstrates.

Completion of design is a critical quality review point.

CASE STUDY 10: TETON DAM – DESIGN UNFIT FOR PURPOSE (ADAPTED FROM BUREAU OF RECLAMATION – ONLINE)

The **Teton Dam**, an earth dam in Idaho, collapsed in 1976 when filling for the first time, killing 11 people and many thousands of cattle, wiping out the town of Wilford completely and severely damaging the city of Rexburg. The dam construction itself had cost over US$40 million; total damage may have been as high as US$2 billion. The dam was not rebuilt nor was one of the railway lines destroyed by the flood water.

The collapse was blamed on inadequate design (a single water-resistant grout curtain to prevent permeation by water), permeable material used for the core and the fissured geology underpinning the dam, allowing undermining of the foundations. The investigation found traces of poor quality construction too. Water seepage led to internal erosion, possibly hydraulic fracturing, and collapse.

The panel investigating the cause of the failure concluded, 'The fundamental cause of failure may be regarded as a combination of geological factors and design decisions that, taken together, permitted the failure to develop.'

This Case study highlights a disaster resulting from elements that were not fit for purpose:

- The site had major flaws that needed major work to make it suitable for a dam.
- The design of the dam was not suitable for its location nor the material used.
- Construction may not have been up to required standards, compounding the problem.

5.3.5 Delivery stage: build

Having designed the solution, it must then be built.

Table 5.6 illustrates the quality documentation and tools used in this project phase.

The products/deliverables and any interim work-pieces or components are tested against the design specification, using the quality methods, standards and tolerances defined for this work. In this phase the components are tested in isolation – testing them together has to wait until integration and commissioning (unless an Agile approach is being used).

A major risk during the build phase is that construction does not follow the original design documentation. This can have major consequences if not managed correctly. Change control is therefore a key quality tool, illustrated by case studies 11 and 12.

Quality and approval records

Clear recording of evidence that all planned quality activities were carried out, and what their results were, provides assurance that (adapted from PRINCE2):

- Products are complete, fit for purpose and compliant with requirements.
- Corrective actions have been requested and completed for any defects found.

TABLE 5.6 Quality Outputs and Tools of Build

Quality outputs	Quality tools used and maintained	
• Test and Inspection Results	• Project Change Control	• Quality Methods defined (supplier)
• Corrective Action Requests	• Project Quality Plan/ Quality Management Strategy	• Product Acceptance Test Plans
• Quality records	• Project Quality Register	• Supplier quality plans
• Change Requests	• Product Descriptions/ Requirements	• Specifications and tolerances
	• Product Acceptance Criteria	• Contract
	• Product Quality Criteria	
	• Standards applied to Products	• Design Documentation
		• Product Quality Criteria (for components)
	• Quality Methods defined	• Quality Methods (for components)
	• Agreed Product Quality Responsibilities	• Test/Inspection Plans
	• Standards applied to supplied Products	• Test/Inspection Equipment

CASE STUDY 11: HYATT REGENCY HOTEL WALKWAY COLLAPSE (ASCE, 2007)

Hyatt Regency hotel, Kansas City, July 1981: the collapse of suspended walkways killed 114 people and injured 216 others. The hotel had a tall atrium crossed by three 137m long, 29 tonne walkways supported from the ceiling. The level 4 walkway was directly above, and suspending, that on level 2.

During construction, a design change added shear load to the fourth-floor walkway's support beams they were not designed for, as a result of construction constraints. The revised design was barely capable of supporting the deadweight of the structure. The added weight of people on the walkways during a big event caused structural failure, and the fourth-floor walkway tore free, falling onto the second-floor walkway, both then falling onto the crowds below, resulting in large-scale death and injury. The critical design change and its unforeseen loading and shear stress consequences are shown in Figure 5.2.

The engineer of record, accountable for the design, reported that one of his subordinates had provisionally approved, by telephone, a design change requested by the fabricator, on condition that a paper-based request was submitted for detailed examination and formal approval. This submission was never made. In a fatal breakdown of communication, the fabricator's sub-contractor, believing the design change had been approved, simply built it without applying their own critical review. Approval of the design drawings was rushed through without examining the details of the redesign. The engineer of record was suspended from the American Society of Civil Engineers for three years for his oversight.

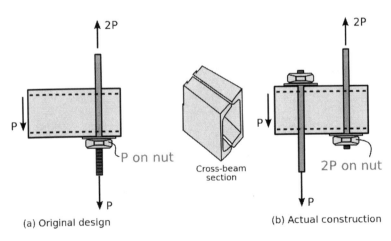

FIGURE 5.2 Faulty redesign at Hyatt Regency, public domain image by 'DTR'

Quality management throughout the project lifecycle **73**

CASE STUDY 12: NUCLEAR FACILITY SEISMIC CERTIFICATION

A European company was contracted to design and build a nuclear facility in the USA. As the area in which the facility was being built is seismically active, a critical safety requirement was the seismic certification of the structural steelwork. The steelwork was designed and the design documentation sent to the regulatory authority for approval, which was duly given.

On completion of the steelwork erection, the regulator inspected it. To the inspectors' concern, the steelwork constructed did not match the approved design. On investigation, it proved that the construction teams had ignored the approved design documentation and built the steelwork to a pattern they had employed successfully in Europe. Work on construction had to cease immediately, given that the steelwork erected was not certified. The project was faced with two options:

- Tear down the steelwork and start again from scratch, this time building to the approved design.
- Reverse-engineer design documentation from the actual steelwork and seek approval from the regulator for the existing construction.

The impact of the first option, both in time and cost, was huge and pushed the project outside tolerance, although it was low risk. The second option was potentially much quicker and cheaper, but higher risk because the existing steelwork may not have been certifiable. If not certifiable, further time would have been lost and option one would have to be followed anyway. Failure to follow approved design documentation was potentially catastrophic for this project.

- Correct processes have been followed and the right people approved the products.
- Any planned audits have been carried out.

These records are used to update the Quality Register entries. During the project, and particularly at final acceptance of the whole project, the quality records ratify the progress made, and feed into learning from experience and improving processes.

Confirmation that quality criteria have been met for all products due for delivery is a critical element of stage gate reviews, allowing the project to progress to the next stage, and any contingent stage payments to be made. Product approval needs to be recorded formally, especially when a payment is to be made, consistent with the QMSs involved.

74 Quality management throughout the project lifecycle

TABLE 5.7 Quality Outputs and Tools of Acceptance

Quality outputs	Quality tools used and maintained	
• Acceptance Test Reports • Corrective Action Requests • Product Acceptance Records • Change Requests	• Project Change Control • Project Quality Requirements • Project Acceptance Criteria • Project Quality Plan/Quality Management Strategy • Project Quality Register • Product Descriptions/Requirements • Product Acceptance Criteria • Product Quality Criteria • Standards applied to Products • Quality Methods defined • Agreed Product Quality Responsibilities • Standards applied to supplied Products	• Quality Methods defined (supplier) • Product Acceptance Test Plans • Supplier quality plans • Specifications and tolerances • Contract • Design Documentation • Product Quality Criteria (for components) • Quality Methods (for components) • Test/Inspection Plans • Test/Inspection Equipment • Test and Inspection Results • Quality records

5.3.6 Delivery stage: acceptance

Project progress is measured by the acceptance of built elements as they are completed. Table 5.7 illustrates the quality documentation and tools used in this project phase.

Where appropriate, testing should include baselining of performance before the project makes changes, so the improvement in performance can be measured and the achievement of the contractual targets confirmed.

However, acceptance testing does not provide a guarantee of the correct outcome. Test plans cannot be exhaustive and are normally risk-based, designed to test thinly around the extremes and focus most of the effort in normal operating conditions. Failures can occur in conditions outside reasonable conditions, or in conditions not recognised at all in the requirements. To illustrate this, 'rogue waves' – giant waves higher than some ships, were regarded as mythical – sailors' tales, like sea serpents and mermaids – until their existence was confirmed in 1995 by the detection of one, 25.9m (85 feet) high, by the Draupner E gas production installation off the coast of Norway (Røsjø & Hauge, 2011). In 2000, a British oceanographic research vessel confirmed, with detailed measurements, a wave 29m (95 feet) high. Subsequent studies using satellite radar measurement of wave height has shown that they are surprisingly common (NY Times, 2006). As these waves are powerful enough to sink some ships, ship design requirements, particularly for bulk carriers, have been changed to cope with them. (IMO, 2004).

Confirmation that quality criteria have been met for all products due is a critical element of their successful acceptance.

Quality management throughout the project lifecycle **75**

TABLE 5.8 Quality Outputs and Tools of Integration and Commissioning

Quality outputs	Quality tools used and maintained	
• Test Reports (Integration)	• Project Change Control	• Product Acceptance Test Plans
• Corrective Action Requests	• Project Quality Plan/Quality Management Strategy	• Supplier quality plans
• Test Records	• Project Quality Register	• Specifications and tolerances
• Product Acceptance Records	• Product Descriptions/ Requirements	• Contract
• Change Requests	• Product Acceptance Criteria	• Design Documentation
	• Product Quality Criteria	• Product Quality Criteria (for components)
	• Standards applied to Products	• Quality Methods (for components)
	• Quality Methods defined	• Test/Inspection Plans
	• Agreed Product Quality Responsibilities	• Test/Inspection Equipment
	• Standards applied to supplied Products	• Test and Inspection Results
	• Quality Methods defined (supplier)	• Quality records

5.3.7 Delivery stage: integration and commissioning

The complete project output/solution has to be assembled, sub-systems integrated and the whole commissioned into usable condition.

Table 5.8 illustrates the quality documentation and tools used in this project phase.

Integration and commissioning are challenging stages for quality control, as large numbers of products are brought together to form complicated systems. The test plans for this phase need to consider complex scenarios and end-to-end operations.

As a late stage in the project life cycle, integration is frequently under time pressure from earlier slippages. By this stage of the project, exhaustive testing is rarely possible; a risk-based approach to selecting the scenarios tested becomes vital. Unfortunately, restricting the scope of testing to save time can exclude improbable but severe scenarios where multiple small failures concatenate to bring the whole solution down.

During integration, there is also the risk that testing can interfere with live systems – particular care and attention is essential in preventing this. Comic author and actor Spike Milligan, in his memoirs, admits creating an invasion scare in Southern England by omitting the heading EXERCISE from a signal he sent reporting an invasion force in the English Channel. A more recent, and very high profile, example is in Case study 13.

76 Quality management throughout the project lifecycle

CASE STUDY 13: HEATHROW TERMINAL 5 – INTEGRATION TESTING INADEQUATE

Heathrow Terminal 5 opened to passengers on 27 March 2008. Over the following 10 days, 42,000 bags went adrift, and over 500 flights were cancelled at a loss to British Airways (BA) of £16 million, with enormous reputational damage. British Airways was only able to operate from Terminal 5 as planned from 8 April 2008 and postponed the move of long-haul flights to T5. Computer Weekly (2008) attributes the difficulties to:

- a lack of IT systems integration testing
- poor preparation of staff and their supporting facilities.

Integration testing 'filters' in the new software (to isolate it from Heathrow's live systems) were accidentally left in place, so T5 systems did not recognise bags transferring from other airlines and sent them for manual sorting.

The integration of the baggage-handling system and baggage reconciliation system didn't work, and staff were unable to log in to sort out issues manually.

Bags missed their flights because staff couldn't see that they had been security screened. Flight data errors prevented the system recognising some bags, which were held back for manual sorting. Wi-Fi problems disabled handheld scanners.

As these errors built up, the baggage-handling system log-jammed, so managers had to switch off the automated re-booking system, creating knock-on problems.

BA blamed inadequate integration testing, caused by delays to construction work, delaying the start of testing. To meet the target opening date, several trials were cancelled, as BA elected to reduce the scope of system trials rather than slip the opening date of the Terminal.

Reflective exercise: should the opening have been delayed instead, or a piloting approach taken, with just a few flights moved to the new terminal to prove it all worked, on a scale at which failure would have been manageable?

5.4 Hand-over/take-over/go-live stage

When commissioning is complete, the customer can take over the solution and put it into live operation.

Table 5.9 illustrates the quality elements created and tools used in this project phase.

Quality management throughout the project lifecycle **77**

TABLE 5.9 Quality Outputs and Tools of Take-over

Quality outputs	*Quality tools used and maintained*	
• Acceptance Test Reports (Final) • Corrective Action Requests • Change Requests • Test Records • Project Acceptance Records	• Project Quality Requirements • Project Acceptance Criteria • Project Quality Plan/ Quality Management Strategy • Project Quality Register • Project Acceptance Test Plans • Product Quality Criteria • Standards applied to Products • Quality Methods defined	• Agreed Product Quality Responsibilities • Standards applied to supplied Products • Specifications and tolerances • Contract • Design Documentation • Test and Inspection Results • Quality records

Final take-over by the client needs prior confirmation that all approvals have been given and recorded for operational, audit and/or contractual purposes. Acceptance may be required from multiple stakeholders, e.g. users and maintainers.

If there are minor faults or non-conformances, acceptance may be given but qualified, with 'concessions' documented. With concessions, it is likely that corrective actions will be mandated. These need to be followed up to ensure they happen in a timely way.

Confirmation that quality criteria have been met for all products is a critical element of handover, and is needed before project closure can take place.

5.5 Benefits realisation stage: warranty, operations and maintenance

Quality requirements for live operations:

- Operations manuals and procedures.
- Maintenance manuals and procedures.
- Training packages.

Human factors are a major contributor to system failures; operator errors in response to unexpected (and untrained-for) circumstances lead to situations never envisaged during the design.

Examples of this include:

- Three Mile Island: the main reactor feed pump failed, the emergency feed pump flow was not routed correctly and poor instrumentation led to operator errors, resulting in the worst nuclear incident in US history (see more detail in Chapter 6).

- Air France A330 AF447 crashed into the South Atlantic; all three pitot heads (which measure airspeed) iced up and the flight control system crashed, bombarding the pilots with error messages – they had still not got on top of the situation when they hit the sea (see more detail in Chapter 10).

These problems all occurred during service, but the roots of these lie in design failures – not considering the operators and maintainers as part of the system/solution.

The warranty period is likely to be the first opportunity to test the validity of operations and maintenance documentation. As this is the last opportunity to get the suppliers to make changes without significant additional expense, it should be seized, testing as intensively as possible.

An example of poor warranty quality occurred at a large off-shore wind farm; very high failure rates during warranty made it obvious that certain components were unfit for purpose. Its owner requested the supplier to replace all those poor-quality components whether they had failed or not. Unfortunately, the terms of the warranty were 'fix on fail'; the supplier stuck to the contract terms, and the turbines continued to fail past the end of warranty.

5.5.1 Decommissioning stage

Decommissioning is rarely considered in the requirements laid down for a project – almost invariably, it's a separate project. Arguably, this puts decommissioning as a phase outside the scope of project quality management. However, those teams trying to dismantle the UK's Magnox nuclear reactors would be delighted if decommissioning had been included in the quality management scope for their construction. Dismantling the result of the project is rarely the reverse of assembling it. Automotive manufacturers are now being forced to design their products for recycling when scrapped.

The challenge is that decommissioning is normally outside the project manager's remit, but ignoring it during design and build can result in hugely increased decommissioning costs.

5.6 Conclusions of chapter

This chapter describes when the key 'tools' of project quality management are applied during the project lifecycle, and what they achieve. It shows how the tools and techniques of quality build progressively on each other as the project progresses.

If we consider the high-level view of what constitutes success as a quality output, quality planning starts with the concept of the project.

It shows how early planning for fitness for purpose and meeting requirements feeds through the lifecycle, reducing subsequent errors. As these errors are a principal source of waste, this reduces waste (hence cost) and reduces the delays stemming from rework.

As each stage builds on the outputs of the earlier stages, from concept, through definition and delivery to hand-over, the priority must be to ensure that adequate quality planning takes place at the start of the project, to provide the firm foundations for the later stages. Cutting investment in, or rushing, quality planning at the start of the project will have progressively more severe consequences the further the project progresses.

5.7 Bibliography

'Achieving Excellence in Construction', No 6 Risk and Value Management, HMSO, London: http://webarchive.nationalarchives.gov.uk/20110622151127/http://www.ogc.gov.uk/ppm_documents_construction.asp

ASCE (2007) – http://www.asce.org/question-of-ethics-articles/jan-2007/

Cartlidge, D. (2003) 'Procurement of Built Assets', Routledge, ISBN: 9780750658195

Computer Weekly (2008) – http://www.computerweekly.com/news/2240086013/British-Airways-reveals-what-went-wrong-with-Terminal-5

IMO (2004) 'Bulk Carrier Safety' – http://www.imo.org/fr/OurWork/Safety/Regulations/Pages/BulkCarriers.aspx

Inc. Magazine (1989) – https://www.inc.com/magazine/19890401/5602.html

NAO (2001) – https://www.nao.org.uk/report/the-millennium-dome/

NY Times (2006) 'Rogue Giants at Sea' – http://www.nytimes.com/2006/07/11/science/11wave.html?ei=5090&en=d5cdc1cbc2182342&ex=1310270400&partner=rssuserland&emc=rss&pagewanted=print&_r=0

PRINCE2 (2009) 'Managing Successful Projects with PRINCE2®' 2009 Edition, Axelos Ltd, ISBN: 9780113310593

Bureau of Reclamation (online) – https://www.usbr.gov/pn/snakeriver/dams/uppersnake/teton/index.html

Røsjø, B. and Hauge, K. (2011) – http://sciencenordic.com/proof-monster-waves-are-real

Further reading – design

Mooz, H., Horsberg, K. and Cotterman, H. (2003) 'Communicating Project Management: The Integrated Vocabulary of Project Management and Systems Engineering', Wiley, Hoboken, NJ, ISBN: 0-471-26924-7

Further reading – design

Davies, A. and Hobday, M. (2009) 'The Business of Projects', Cambridge University Press, Cambridge ISBN: 9780511493294

Gardiner, P. D. (2005) 'Project Management: A Strategic Planning Approach', Palgrave Macmillan, Basingstoke ISBN: 9780333982228

6

WHERE DOES QUALITY NEED MANAGING?

Reflective exercise: if you need a quality focus at all times, what environments do you need to be getting things right in? How can you make things easier for yourself?

This chapter explains that quality management thinking must be applied in all the key project-related environments:

- in the office
- in the factory
- on the operational site.

It describes the key distractions from quality working in each of these environments, including being asked to work quicker, using less resource (the result of the correct balance between time, cost and quality not being identified correctly).

It offers suggestions on how to address these environmental distractions.

Learning outcomes for the chapter

After reading this chapter, the reader should understand:

- How quality activities vary by location.
- The barriers to achieving quality working.
- Tools and techniques for making quality working easier, and a way of life.

6.1 In the office

In the early stages of projects most, if not all, of the work is in the office environment, and much of the project management remains there throughout. In software development projects, the office is the 'factory floor'. People work at their desks, have meetings and use computer workstations in the office.

The office environment can feel isolated from the reality of construction and engineering projects, so it can be difficult to stay focused on quality all the time, at the desk, in meetings, doing paperwork and communicating.

6.1.1 At the desk

At the desk, there are many distractions from getting everything right, including:

- Tight time pressures.
- Poor time management – overloading.
- Poor prioritisation.
- Fire-fighting.

There are several things make quality working easier, including:

- Easy access to documentation.
- Easy access to standards and other references.
- An encouraging atmosphere and good time management creating time to get things right.

IT systems supporting quality management

Virtually any aspect of quality management benefits from effective IT support. A desk is very likely to have a computer on it, making access to IT systems quick and easy. Access to IT systems away from the desk depends on the technology available, particularly the availability of wireless networks and mobile devices.

6.1.2 In the meeting room

Meetings can make or break a quality culture. Human interaction can make life sparkle, work interesting and people energetic; the human interaction in meetings can either harness that energy or suppress it. There are important distractions from quality working in meetings:

- Too many meetings – no time to do the work.
- Too many people in meetings, leading to protracted discussions.
- Meetings too long – poor time/agenda management.
- Lack of focus – participants distracted by checking e-mails, writing documents or other activities not necessary for the meeting.
- Lack of preparation for meetings – preparation has to be done **during** the meeting.

82 Where does quality need managing?

There are useful aids to quality working in meetings:

- Minimise the number of meetings – limit them to achieving agreement where it can't be achieved without debate.
- Having a tailored agenda, focused on successful outcomes.
- Tight time management of meetings.
- Prompt production and publishing of notes from meetings, especially actions.
- Attendance limited to those actively involved.
- Preparation before the meeting.

To increase the effectiveness of time invested in meetings, always check the purpose of the meeting, and why you are being invited:

- What will **you** contribute to the meeting? If you will not be making a significant contribution, decline the invitation and ask to be informed of the outcome.
- Can your input be provided up front rather than during the meeting? If so, decline to attend.
- Can multiple meetings be combined?
- Ask who else will be going – can someone deputise for you? If so, decline to attend.
- Only accept 'for information only' if it is a briefing session for that purpose.
- Always prepare for the meeting – know the agenda and target outcomes. Request and read the material to be considered BEFORE the meeting – you may decide not to go after all.
- For quality reviews, adopt a standard approach.

Meetings are there to deliver results, not to waste time.

6.1.3 Doing the paperwork

Every project requires documentation, irrespective of the methodology employed and the type of project. Quality documentation is particularly vital as it enables acceptance, approval, hand-over and finally project closure, not to mention payment.

There are people who delight in documentation, and they have a vital function within the project organisation in helping everyone else to create and maintain the records necessary. Most people working on a project do **not** delight in documenting; they see it as standing in the way of achieving their targets, rather than facilitating it. This very human viewpoint has to be addressed.

The QMS must provide the **minimum acceptable level** of documentation, to avoid unnecessary overhead. The wrong way to do this is for the people who love paperwork to design the QMS, leaving it for the people who hate paperwork

Where does quality need managing? **83**

to operate it. The optimum level can only be achieved by team working between those producing, and those using, the quality paperwork. Distractions from maintaining quality documentation include:

- Too much documentation – too time-consuming and tedious to complete.
- Duplication of details between forms.
- Value not obvious – doesn't seem a priority.
- Other people don't handle documents in a timely way – delays, backlogs.

Aids to maintaining quality paperwork include:

- Records tailored to the needs of the people completing it – engage with the stakeholders to determine their requirements.
- Simplified, targeted forms – quick to complete with obvious value. Use IT – forms designed to minimise data entry.
- Minimise the number of steps/reviewers to streamline the process. Use IT – workflow instead of e-mail or internal post.
- Regular audit to prevent backlogs building up. Use IT – track performance of processing quality documentation.

6.1.4 On the telephone, e-mail and other remote forms of communication

Quality management is critically dependent on effective communications. In the project environment, a wide range of mechanisms are available – using the right blend of these ensures fully-shared understanding of quality information.

Table 6.1 shows how information content varies dramatically with the communication method used.

Face-to-face discussions and text messaging can both be appropriate in different contexts. However, using an inappropriate means of communication can dramatically reduce the effectiveness of the message. A key point is that e-mails, especially if short and poorly thought-out, are a very poor channel of communication for tasking people in the first place. The recipient can't tell the urgency and sincerity of your tasking, and the sender can't tell whether the message has been fully understood and a commitment made. The most reliable tasking is face-to-face with supporting written information for reference that clearly details what is to be done.

As human beings are primates, our primary sense is vision, and most people prefer communication through visual means (they **see** what you mean). However, a significant minority of people prefer auditory communication (they **hear** what you say), and some prefer kinaesthetic (they **feel** they know what you want) communication.

The effectiveness of your choice of words and communications channels depends on the preference of the recipient.

TABLE 6.1 Tasking for quality – communications channels

Mechanism	Information Content						
	Body language	Facial Expression	Vocal expression	Real-time response	Pictures	Detailed text	Brief text
Face to Face briefings/conversations	Y	Y	Y	Y	Y		Y
1:1 video conferencing		Y	Y	Y	Y		Y
Room–wide VC			Y	Y			
Telephone			Y	Y			
Documents					Y	Y	Y
E-mails (excludes attachments)						½	Y
MMS					Y		Y
TXT							Y

Information towards the left is vital for communicating:

- Urgency, importance and sincerity
- Whether the message is getting through and being understood

Whether there is commitment to doing what is required

Information towards the right is vital for communicating:

- Exactly what must be done,
- When it has been done

6.2 The factory production environment – creating quality products

Many projects involve the manufacture of physical items in factories, such as valves, girders, chemicals, paper, furniture etc. so the factory is a significant location for project quality management in many cases. Where software is being created, the 'factory floor' is an office environment, but delivering quality products requires the same disciplines as in a conventional factory. As quality management was born in the production environment, here we will focus just on the project-supplier relationship.

Distractions from quality production include:

- Inaccurate or ambiguous requirements, leading to inadequate designs.
- Unnecessarily tight tolerances specified, beyond the supplier's normal capability.
- Poor quality management by the supplier, both in-house and of their own supply chain.
- Inadequate change control by the project and/or the supplier.
- Unviably low profit margin driving cost- and corner-cutting by the supplier.

Aids to quality in production include:

- A close working relationship with the customer allowing clarification of design issues (technical queries), backed up by rigorous change control.
- Clear and unambiguous design documentation resulting from clear and unambiguous requirements.
- Achievable design tolerances being agreed by the supplier through the design review process.
- A fair profit margin for the supplier without compromising quality.

IT aids to quality on the shop floor

There may be conventional desktop computers available on the shop floor, and control systems can usually collect data relating to quality. There is a wide range of wireless, portable, handheld commercial and industrial IT devices available, from radio frequency identification (RFID) and barcode scanners for tracking items, through Smart Phones to tablets, like the Apple iPad or Microsoft Surface.

These mostly exploit wireless networking advances (Wi-Fi and 3/4G). The most obvious challenge for mobile devices remains battery life, although this is improving. Key factors in suitability of a device include:

- Versatility (operating system).
- Size of screen (information display capability).
- Input devices (keyboard/stylus/finger/voice).

86 Where does quality need managing?

- Network connectivity.
- Ease of hand-held use.

The device market is constantly changing, but:

- Tablets e.g. iPad and convertibles e.g. MS Surface are very versatile:
  - Large display, for rich information display.
  - Powerful operating system offering capabilities close to a desktop.
  - Too large to fit in a pocket, reducing easy portability.
- Smartphones:
  - Smaller display size, but growing.
  - Limited operating system – limited functionality.
  - Bespoke apps easy – tailoring for specific tasks quite practical.
  - Handy size, fit in pockets.
- Tailored device e.g. barcode scanner, ruggedised laptop:
  - Task-specific.
  - Performance optimised for environment.
  - High purchase cost due to niche market.

> *Reflective exercise: where have you seen mobile IT used to deliver quality, in everyday life and in projects? Where else could it be used to good advantage?*

6.2.1 The factory test environment

Quite obviously, this is a vitally important area for project quality – it is the last point where the project has the opportunity to reject a product as unfit before its delivery to the site.

Testing by the supplier is vitally important and so is factory acceptance testing by the project.

The following all distract from testing quality:

- Acceptance criteria are not clear and unambiguous – test plans not well-defined or thorough enough.
- Test equipment is inappropriate – either in capability or scope.
- The culture is 'nearly right is good enough'.
- There is a track record of accepting products just outside tolerance/specification.
- Access of project/customer staff to the test site is difficult or expensive.

The following all help in delivering quality:

- Very clear acceptance criteria.
- A close working relationship between project staff and supplier staff.
- Appropriate equipment for factory acceptance test.
- Clear and detailed factory acceptance test plans.

Where does quality need managing? **87**

- Audit reports, confirming the quality management system is measuring conformance effectively.
- Interim test reports, with analysis and summary showing whether the requirements have been met.

6.3 On site

On the final site of the project, as well as offices, there may be goods reception areas, test/inspection areas, training facilities and the construction site itself (although these may be virtual environments for software projects). Once the solution goes live, there is the operational environment which also requires maintenance.

6.3.1 Quality delivery into integration/commissioning

Distractions from quality in integration and commissioning include:

- Components/material/products delivered late.
- Components/material/products not correctly identified/labelled.
- Components/Products that fail on-site testing or inspection or do not fit.
- Contractual issues over non-conformances.
- Skilled manpower not available at the right time.
- Right equipment not available at the right time, e.g. Crane, server environment.
- Inadequate quality plans for the testing and inspection.
- Breakdown of effective team-working between different parties.

Aids to quality integration and commissioning include:

- Accurate project plan easily available, showing latest updated delivery dates.
- Clear and practical quality plans for integration and commissioning.
- Unambiguous product IDs used consistently across all parties, labelling the products themselves.
- Readily-available factory acceptance test results.
- Detailed manpower and skills plan with adequate capacity to handle minor problems.
- Accountable personnel clearly identified for all activities, especially quality activities.
- An effective team spirit, focused on winning together, across all parties involved.
- Zero tolerance for 'blame storms', the project team focuses on solving the problem rather than arguing over who is to blame for it.

6.3.2 Quality in operation

Once the project has delivered the solution, the balance tilts from investment to payback. Quality in the operation of the solution is necessary to deliver economic operation and the target business benefits, and to achieve the expected lifespan.

88 Where does quality need managing?

Distractions from quality operation include:

- Complacency by operational/maintenance staff or management, leading to skimping and short-cuts in the maintenance/operational care of the solution.
- Carelessness, leading to accidents.
- Confusing/clumsy/annoying/irritating user interface leading to operator errors.
- Operational incidents occurring outside the design scope.
- Operational incidents occurring outside the training scope.

Aids to quality operation include:

- Good, clear, concise standard operating procedures, kept up to date.
- Comprehensive disaster management plans, kept up to date with exercises and risk workshops.
- Ergonomically designed user interfaces.
- Up to date training material for new operators.
- Mandatory training of all new operators.
- Mandatory refresher training for existing operators.

Case study 14 illustrates how a number of relatively small failures compounded, each resulting from quality failures during the life of the project, and a nuclear disaster was only narrowly avoided in the USA.

Chernobyl, for similar reasons, went one step further, exploded in Ukraine, and influenced the whole world's attitude towards nuclear power.

CASE STUDY 14: THREE MILE ISLAND NUCLEAR INCIDENT

28th March 1979 saw a partial core meltdown at Three Mile Island Nuclear Generating Station in Pennsylvania. The pumps circulating water through the secondary cooling loop of the reactor failed (see Figure 6.1). The operators misinterpreted the situation and took actions that resulted in radioactive material escaping into the containment building. Fortunately, no one was injured, and there were no detectable effects to the environment or population.

The Event Sequence:

At 4.00 a.m. the main feedwater pump failed, reducing cooling flow to the primary heat exchanger. The backup feedwater pump should have started, but after recent testing, the workers had forgotten to realign the valves, so the secondary couldn't take over. The primary coolant heated up, raising its pressure. To reduce the pressure, the pilot-operated relief valve (PORV) opened. The PORV was supposed to close when the pressure in the reactor dropped; it did not, leading to steam and water venting into the containment building.

Where does quality need managing? **89**

The control panel had an indicator that showed a close command had been sent to the valve but there was nothing to reveal the valve's **actual** position, leaving the operators unaware of the open valve.

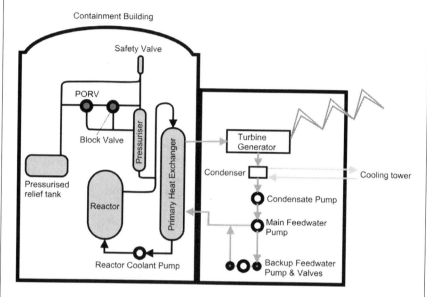

FIGURE 6.1 Three Mile Island schematic – adapted from the US Nuclear Regulatory Commission (US NRC)

With the uncontrolled venting, reactor pressure dropped and the water in the reactor boiled, further increasing the overheating problem; the temperature in the exposed part of the core reached 2,370°C, dangerously close to meltdown, but the operators were unaware, believing that the core was covered and safe. The system was supposed to be fail-safe – it wasn't, so it had not met its requirements.

There were design flaws, stopping the systems from being fail-safe:

- The PORV failed to close after relieving excess pressure in the system.
- The emergency water pump valves could be left misaligned after a test.

User Interface design flaws led to the operators being misled:

- No indication to the operators that the relief valve was still open.
- No instruments indicating core coolant level to the operators.

90 Where does quality need managing?

Operator training failures led to human errors:

- The operators made a number of incorrect diagnoses of the situation that led to errors
- No rehearsal of a major incident of this nature had been held

6.3.3 Quality in maintenance

Maintenance is the main activity that ensures delivery of the lifetime business benefit originally envisaged. The return on the initial investment can be massively compromised by poor maintenance.

Factors that could distract from the quality of maintenance include:

- Maintenance staff are inadequately trained.
- Wrong tooling and equipment are supplied, resulting in damage and accidents or time wasted finding the correct tooling.
- Documentation and reality have drifted apart – standard operating procedures (SOPs) and other documentation have not been updated in line with the equipment/plant.
- No support for old (obsolete) equipment is available from suppliers.

Aids to good quality maintenance include:

- Standard operating procedures (SOPs) for all maintenance tasks are readily available and kept up to date.
- All maintenance staff are trained appropriately.
- Maintenance contracts are in place for equipment that will be difficult to maintain with in-house skills.
- Maintenance tooling and equipment is fit for purpose and well-maintained.
- Up to date design documentation is readily available.
- Easy access to original equipment supplier (if still in business) and expert substitute supplier (if not) assured contractually.
- Maintenance schedule includes all activities by all maintenance staff, internal and external.
- Maintenance schedule is managed to minimise loss from outages.

6.4 Conclusions of chapter

This chapter concludes that quality management thinking has to be applied in all the key project environments, in the office, in the factory and on the operational site.

Of these environments, the office is particularly important; this is where most quality planning is carried out, and most of the paperwork. People working in the office can feel isolated from the reality of the project, especially if it is a major construction or other engineering project.

Working on the operational site (even if it is an IT project) is also a challenge for quality management, as the reality of a construction site or contact centre can seem very remote from the office environment in which quality was planned.

This chapter offers suggestions on how to address effectively the key distractions from quality working in each of these environments.

It identifies how not correctly balancing the triangle between time, cost and quality can create pressures that damage the project.

6.5 Bibliography

US NRC – https://www.nrc.gov/reading-rm/doc-collections/fact-sheets/3mile-isle.html

7

EXTENDING QUALITY MANAGEMENT THROUGH THE SUPPLY CHAIN

This chapter probes the impact on projects of good planning and control of quality management in the supply chain, and considers the synergies possible between procurement processes and supply chain quality. This involves considering quality as a key element of procurement and not just buying from whichever supplier can offer the lowest purchase price.

It considers the benefits of supplier auditing, clear requirements documentation and clearly-defined acceptance criteria. It goes on to consider the value of supplier approval for contract quality plans and use of third party inspection bodies.

It then looks into the types of relationships with suppliers, supplier development as a quality improvement strategy, and use of quality incentives, to drive project cost reductions and timeliness.

Learning outcomes for the chapter

After reading this chapter, the reader should understand:

- The impact of customer/supplier relationships on quality.
- Tools and techniques for improving supply chain quality.
- The project is **accountable** for project quality, although the supply chain has responsibilities.

7.1 Introduction to supply chain quality

It is easy to pick the cheap option in sourcing material and components for projects, as this appears to reduce the forecast project costs. However, a consequent quality failure can drive up costs far more than was saved.

Ron Baden Hellard (Hellard, 1993) championed the need for quality management in construction projects to overcome their record of delivering poor quality, resulting from fragmentation of the supply chain.

Researching into construction projects, Karim, Marosszeky and Davis (2006) unsurprisingly concluded that quality management of the subcontractor supply chain is critical to achieving quality and reducing the incidence of defects.

It is not just construction projects that suffer if the supply chain delivers poor quality. The following extended case study illustrates the lethal consequences which can result from poor supply chain quality management in aerospace.

7.1.1 Supply chain quality malfunction – Space Shuttle Challenger disaster

The first Space Shuttle disaster occurred on January 28, 1986, when the Shuttle Challenger started to disintegrate 73 seconds after lift-off; the final crash killed all its crew. The supply chain involved NASA Marshall Space Center (the project manager), Rockwell International (the prime contractor for the Shuttle itself) and Morton Thiokol, the manufacturers of the solid rocket boosters (SRBs).

The problem began when a seal between sections of the right SRB failed at lift-off; leaking hot gas cut through supports and the main tank, causing its disintegration in ball of flame and the crash of the Shuttle orbiter vehicle with the crew on board.

The Rogers Commission's investigation (Rogers Commission, 1986) found that NASA managers had known since 1977 that the SRBs contained this potentially catastrophic flaw, but had not resolved it. They had also overruled engineers' warnings about the risk posed to the seals from the low temperatures on that morning.

Pre-launch conditions and delay

Challenger's launch was delayed by various factors by nearly a week, building pressure to launch without further delay.

At $-1°C$, the forecast for 28 January was the minimum temperature permitted for launch by Rockwell. Engineers at Morton Thiokol were concerned about the poor low temperature resilience of the SRBs' joint seals. Each SRB was composed of four sections with three 'field' joints, each sealed by two rubber O-rings, a primary and its backup, to contain the hot gases. Thiokol engineers were not sure the joint would seal properly below $12°C$. With no backup if the O-rings failed, destruction of the Orbiter would be inevitable.

NASA managers argued that if the primary O-ring failed, the secondary O-ring would still seal, overlooking the obvious; if one failed due to the low temperature, both would fail. The Thiokol engineers' argument, that the cold-soak overnight at $-6°C$ would almost certainly result in much lower SRB temperatures than they were designed, for was overruled by Thiokol's own management, influenced by NASA.

94 Extending quality management through the supply chain

The engineers at Rockwell were alarmed by the level of ice at the launch pad. They feared ice damage during launch and advised Rockwell's managers at the Cape against a launch. However, their concerns led to just an hour's delay, for another inspection by the Ice Team. Challenger was cleared to launch at 11:38 a.m.

Investigation by Rogers Commission

It emerged after the disaster that, contrary to public perception that NASA operated a safety culture, their managers frequently overrode regulations to maintain launch schedules.

The Rogers Commission found the failure of the O-rings resulted from a design fault, easily compromised by the low temperature on the day of launch.

The report also highlighted the failure of both NASA and Morton Thiokol in accepting the design flaw as a flight risk, rather than a redesign need (a violation of NASA regulations). Even when it was recognised that the flaw was serious, NASA never considered grounding the shuttle to fix the fault.

The U.S. House Committee on Science and Technology agreed with the Rogers Commission as to the technical causes of the accident. However, it differed from the committee in its assessment of the accident's contributing causes, attributing the fundamental problem not to poor communication, but to poor technical decision-making over a period of several years by top NASA and contractor personnel, who failed to solve the faults in the SRB joints.

NASA initiated a total redesign of the SRBs, watched over by an independent group as stipulated by the commission.

Sadly, this quality failure, a design that didn't meet the safety requirements, was just the first Shuttle disaster.

> *Reflective exercise: read the Rogers Commission Report. What are the key learning points from this disaster which can be related to quality management of the project supply chain?*

7.2 Synergies between supplier quality assurance and procurement processes

In contrast to the Challenger story, two Case studies (15 and 16) from the electrical/electronics sectors illustrate the benefit of procurement and supplier quality assurance being aligned — reduction in rate of defects, boosting customer satisfaction, and a reduction in costs due to reduced waste from defects.

> *Reflective exercise: how could some of these principles be applied to the project environment?*

This could include:

- *Detailed quality management of suppliers.*
- *Training suppliers in quality management techniques.*
- *Questioning how suppliers will manage the quality of their sub-contractors.*
- *Encouraging suppliers to aim for right first time, aim for zero 'snagging'.*

CASE STUDY 15: CASCADING QUALITY DOWN THE SUPPLY CHAIN

A provider of electronic radio frequency identification devices (RFID) for stock and document management outsourced all its manufacturing to partners who assemble the products and dispatch them direct to customers. These partners are responsible for ensuring the quality of the products prior to dispatch. One of the partners was beset with quality problems, leading to frequent product recalls, fire-fighting by installation engineers, and unhappy customers.

Investigation and analysis at this partner's premises showed that the largest source of problems was the cabinets which housed the electronics. Dimensional errors, poor paint finish, burrs, sharp edges, misaligned hinges and access ports were commonplace. The partner's staff had been trying to patch up the quality problems in their own premises and occasionally moaning at the cabinet supplier. Instead, it was decided to cascade the quality programme into the 'second tier' suppliers such as the cabinet producer, successfully addressing the problems.

CASE STUDY 16: REPLACING A SUPPLIER WITH A QUALITY SUPPLIER

A company that provides bespoke protection and control equipment for construction engineering projects was also experiencing variable quality product from their cabinet supplier. Their solution was to evaluate a number of potential alternative suppliers and they eventually identified a company who were several years into a quality and productivity improvement programme. After a short period of dual sourcing, it became clear that this company had developed a very impressive manufacturing capability, the quality of their products was very consistent, and, although they weren't the cheapest company in the market, sourcing was quickly switched, with the vast majority of cabinet orders placed with them. The increase in cabinet prices has been covered several times over by reducing the hidden costs associated with constant fire-fighting and corrective actions.

7.3 Use of supplier auditing in quality assurance

Auditing, 'a systematic review or assessment' (Oxford English Dictionary), of quality plays an important role in achieving customer satisfaction, and can be used widely in the project environment, including selection of main contractor, sub-contractors and progress evaluation of sub-contractors. As auditing is carried out to independent standards, it is a powerful tool in identifying the shortfalls in management or production that may lead to defects.

7.3.1 Automotive manufacturing

One of the first industry sectors to introduce auditing as a means of managing supply chain quality was automotive. Toyota led in developing total supply chain quality as part of developing the Toyota production system (which in turn forms the basis of 'Lean thinking', see Womack and Jones, 2003). The five Lean principles are:

- Identify where value lies.
- Map the flow of value through the business as streams.
- Smooth the flow of value, removing blockages and bottlenecks.
- Facilitate 'just in time' pull of value, instead pushing into stockpiles.
- Strive for perfection – eliminate the waste of not getting it right first time.

It was recognised that inspecting-in quality and taking corrective actions is very resource intensive, expensive and can never be 100 per cent reliable. If there is poor quality and variability at the input to a conversion process, it is inevitable that some of this will exit the process.

Auditing of suppliers confirms that their quality management approach assures that quality components will be delivered, by confirming by direct inspection that their quality processes and standards are fit for purpose, that they are being applied and that the people applying them have been suitably trained.

To control supplies of raw materials, components and sub-assemblies, auditing of suppliers became commonplace. In addition, suppliers were encouraged to adopt their own TQM programmes. Tier 1 suppliers were expected to encourage their suppliers (Tier 2) to develop quality programmes in turn, and as part of this, Tier 1 audited Tier 2. Considerable rationalisation of supply chains resulted. The use of this approach has expanded steadily.

7.4 The need for clear requirements documentation

Clearly defined, detailed and documented requirements, under rigorous change management, are an essential component of managing quality and fitness for purpose in project supply chains. The perils of not doing so are illustrated in Case study 17.

CASE STUDY 17: SPECIALITY COATINGS

A speciality paper coating company was upgrading its paper roll handling system, replacing a manual process with automation.

The main contract was awarded to a multinational project engineering company, who in turn sub-contracted the design and build to a specialist supplier, HME. One component was a relatively straight-forward, tried and trusted system but the other required a high level of bespoke design, specific to the plant.

Initially, the project proceeded to plan with good progress on the building modification and infrastructure to house the new system. This included good maintenance of the integrity of the plant as it continued to produce.

However, numerous on-going changes continued long after a design freeze should have been reached. Design input gradually shifted from HME to the paper company, largely due to the personalities involved, and the system became progressively more complicated.

The continuing delays to this (and a larger project for another client) coupled with a downturn in the economy, resulted in a sudden cash flow dip at HME, and insolvency. The paper coating company was warned and extracted the almost complete machinery just ahead of the receivers. There had been no factory acceptance testing; testing couldn't start until the system had been installed in the paper plant several months later.

Testing showed many shortcomings. Initial operating performance was very poor, with very high levels of downtime. Lack of clear requirements or strong change control resulted in four years and many redesigns in operation to achieve downtime performance approaching acceptable levels.

If requirements are unclear, undocumented or uncontrolled, differences between customer expectations and project deliveries are bound to develop, leading to rework and delays and/or customer disappointment.

7.5 The need for clear acceptance criteria

In the early phases of projects, it is usual for much effort to be invested in documenting what is required. Often it is only much later in the project that effort is focused on defining acceptance criteria and acceptance tests. This has two major drawbacks:

- It may not be practicable to test satisfactorily against the requirements provided.
- When the acceptance criteria and tests are finally defined, they may reveal flaws in the requirements.

98 Extending quality management through the supply chain

How can this be addressed? An obvious solution is to define acceptance criteria as part of defining the requirements. This guarantees the requirements are testable, and can be verified, before the contract is placed. Clear and explicit acceptance criteria reduce ambiguity for the supplier, who is then able to design a product capable of being accepted.

Including the acceptance criteria at the requirements stage may well impinge on organisational structural divisions, involving a culture change that is not trivial, and this is highlighted in Case study 18.

CASE STUDY 18: CHEMICAL PLANT PROJECT ACCEPTANCE PROBLEMS

A producer of high-value speciality chemicals contracted with a major multi-national civil engineering contractor to upgrade their solution-handling and mixing plant, for a fixed price.

The process control system was sub-contracted to a large US-based specialist. Clear specifications for plant modes of operation were developed and this included the sequencing required for the process control system, but acceptance test plans were undefined. Extensive plans were also put in place for training staff to operate the plant when it was completed.

The construction of the plant buildings and solution handling equipment proceeded according to plan. However, it emerged that the main contractor's project team had little understanding of how the process control system would work with the plant, and initial trial results did not match the requirements of the customer.

Many months of wrangling followed, with the process control company arguing that their design should be accepted as it met the documented requirements, the customer indicating that the plant was not operable (so not fit for purpose) and the main contractor trying to minimise their cost escalation. All three parties redeployed their project teams until a solution was found.

Eventually, the contractor assigned a project manager to rescue the project and the process control system was extracted from the sub-contractor 'as is' and installed in the new plant, nearly four years late. It then needed substantial further development of the plant sequencing, undertaken by the customer's own electrical engineering design team.

The control systems specialist's lack of access to acceptance criteria and test plans led to them delivering a product that met the specifications, but neither met the requirements nor was fit for purpose.

7.5.1 Service level agreements in accepting services

Acceptance of a service is not just a 'one off' event, but continuous. Where a service is being procured, the minimum acceptable level of performance is often defined through a service level agreement (SLA). SLAs began to emerge in the late 1980s in the IT industry. They formed the performance assessment basis for IT services, originally as a payment mechanism linked to reliability of networks. These performance measures were also linked to penalties for different levels of delivery interruption.

SLAs can also be used for defining, agreeing, managing and reviewing internal customer/supplier relationships within an organisation, e.g. between tendering and contracts departments, between contracts and engineering, etc.

Cousins et al (2008) argue that SLAs can be very difficult to define, particularly in service sectors where the performance is hard to measure. For example, a consultancy may claim to have provided cost saving or productivity improvement services where the fee includes a performance incentive. To what extent have those improvements arisen because of the intervention as opposed to work undertaken by the customer's employees? In addition, how can the baseline for improvement be defined when volume output or sales demand vary? In a manufacturing environment, it can be easier to define an SLA by using readily quantifiable measures such as percentage or parts per million defects, delivery schedule achievement or non-supply of certificates of conformance. Table 7.1 illustrates a simple SLA.

Routine project administrative functions are a promising area for SLAs. One project set a change request processing SLA target as 100 per cent reviewed and 80 per cent addressed within six days, for example.

Reflective exercise: how could SLAs be applied effectively in a project environment?

TABLE 7.1 Example Service Level Agreement (SLA)

An example of a Service Level Agreement (extract)

1. Order confirmation – receipt of order will be confirmed within 24 hours, together with delivery date.
2. Orders will be satisfied within agreed lead time, where these orders are placed according to forecast provided.
3. All delivery windows will be confirmed latest 24 hours before delivery is due.
4. All deliveries will be achieved in the window confirmed.
5. Certificates of Conformance will be provided for all deliveries, either before or with the delivery.
6. Non-conformances will be raised for any out of specification product.

CASE STUDY 19: SMALL CUSTOMER, MINIMAL PURCHASING POWER

A small manufacturer of shower enclosures used coated aluminium profiles bought from a large aluminium extrusion company. The extrusions were delivered with so many defects that all had to be inspected on receipt, and defective profiles rejected, at considerable effort and cost.

The enclosure company had requested improved quality for some time but the aluminium company refused; this application, at the high-quality end of their range, was a small contributor to their total turnover and not worth upgrading their production capabilities to match the requirements.

The product was fit for purpose in the eyes of the large supplier, but not in the eyes of the small customer. The enclosure company investigated switching supplier, but there were no viable alternatives due to global demand and their investment in extrusion dies at the supplier's premises.

This sorry situation is very different to Case study 20.

CASE STUDY 20: LARGE CUSTOMER – CLOSE COLLABORATION

Despite the problems on its opening, Nuno Gil's research on the relationships between BAA and its suppliers in the Heathrow T5 project (Gil, 2009) shows that much of the construction phase was a success. T5 opened on time and on budget on 27 March 2008, a date fixed six years earlier.

BAA fostered relationships with suppliers, advocating:

- Collaborative partnerships.
- Open disclosure of information, including financial costings.
- Continuous improvement.
- Trust building practices, such as transferring employees and guest engineers.
- Sourcing work from fewer but highly competent suppliers, to reduce variability.
- Eliminating non-value-added activities.
- Identifying critical information flows and feedback loops.
- Just in time deliveries to the construction site, together with just in time holding areas for items about to be installed.

BAA hired a firm of consultants specialising in Lean techniques to work with suppliers to improve their productivity and quality.

7.6 Quality needs the right relationship with the suppliers

Chapter 3 described the breakdown of customer-supplier relationships on the Channel Tunnel project. Customer-supplier relationships play a critical role in project success. Case studies 19 and 20 illustrate opposite extremes – 19 describes the uncomfortable scenario where the supplier has all the power and declines to support the customer, and 20 describes a powerful customer electing to support its suppliers to deliver a successful outcome.

7.7 Supplier development improves quality management

Commonly, buyers try to improve suppliers' performance through competitive tendering and use of multiple suppliers. This encourages each supplier to develop their performance in the area sought by the customer, e.g. cost, quality or timeliness.

Supplier development takes a very different approach, with the customer working more collaboratively with fewer suppliers to boost their performance. In supply chains applying Lean principles, it is common for buyer organisations to have direct involvement in suppliers, for example, partial acquisition of supplier firms, equipment capital investment at a supplier and training and skills development.

Krause et al (2000) concluded that the most effective supplier development strategy is direct involvement. They found that other strategies such as incentive schemes or awards tended to have short-term benefits and failed to achieve sustained improvements. Audit visits often leave suppliers with a list of actions which don't get done for various reasons. Success rates are much higher when customers adopt more direct involvement programmes, such as training supplier employees or sending improvement engineers to supplier premises to be directly involved in implementing audit proposals.

It is not possible to justify supplier development relationships with all suppliers, due to time and resource constraints. Some suppliers may already be operating at the right level; spend with others may be too small to warrant such involvement. Hence, prioritisation/selection is needed, based on spend, volume, delivery performance, reliability and the PONC of the things supplied, i.e. lower cost components that could have a huge impact on the project if late or out of specification.

Cousins et al (2008) also consider other factors, such as the likely length of a relationship and prioritising the weakest suppliers for development activities, as this will probably have the most benefit on overall supply chain performance. Creating a supplier base, with fewer suppliers working more closely with the customer to deliver and maintain continuous improvement in the supply chain, boosts quality (as shown in Figure 7.1).

This can be applied to all types of organisations, whether they are manufacturing, project or service-orientated. There is no optimum point shown, but the law of diminishing returns applies, as ultimately too few suppliers limits the ability to deliver.

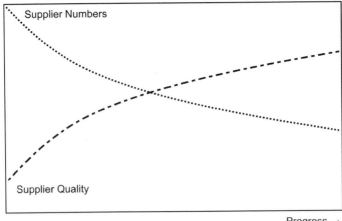

FIGURE 7.1 Return on supplier development

Reflective exercise: could supplier performance be improved by deploying a direct supplier involvement strategy in your working environment?

7.8 Quality incentives

When dealing with subcontractors or other suppliers, what motivates them to deliver to your quality standards? Outside the supplier development model discussed above, there are two basic inducements:

- Quality achievement premiums.
- Quality failure penalties.

They represent the traditional 'carrot and stick'.

7.8.1 Quality achievement premiums

This is the 'carrot'; the supplier is rewarded for delivering to quality standards. The reward may be of several types:

Financial – additional payments are made for achievement of quality standards. Additional payments are justified by the reduction in the price of non-conformance.

Relational – where achievement of quality targets is rewarded by a strengthening of the relationship between the supplier and customer, for example the awarding of preferred supplier status to the supplier or priority when bidding for further work.

Extending quality management through the supply chain **103**

Reputational – where the customer actively publicises the achievements of the supplier in meeting quality standards which benefits the supplier in winning new customers.

The overall quality achievement premium may be a blend of all three.

The message of setting quality achievement premiums is one of trust between the customer and supplier. The relationship between the two parties is one of improving and strengthening, with both parties sharing in the benefits of achievement.

7.8.2 Quality failure penalties

This is the 'stick'; the supplier is penalised for failing to deliver to quality standards. As with the quality achievement premiums, the penalties can take multiple forms:

Financial – financial reparations are required from the supplier to the customer to compensate for the price of non-conformance resulting from their failure to meet quality standards. The scale of these financial reparations must be agreed before placement of the contract.

Relational – failure to meet quality targets means loss of preferred status, future orders and quite possibly reduced tolerance (where there is any degree of ambiguity) around acceptance of the remaining work.

Reputational – where the customer publicises the failure of the supplier to meet quality standards, perhaps through suing, which results in media coverage.

The overall quality failure penalty may be a blend of all three.

The message of setting quality failure penalties can be one of distrust between the customer and supplier. The relationship between the two parties can become one of defensiveness.

7.8.3 Strengths of using premiums and penalties

Careful use of premiums and penalties can help to identify which quality targets and standards are really important. In a strong customer supplier relationship, a good balance between carrot and stick is clearly understood by both parties to be in their mutual interests and to be fair and reasonable. It represents the sharing of risk between the two parties in a clearly defined way.

Case study 21 shows successful use of incentives.

7.8.4 Risks of using premiums and penalties

Ill-thought-through use of premiums and penalties can distract the supplier from the true priorities. Punitive damages clauses in contracts can delay the agreement and even break the deal. Overgenerous quality premiums not tightly focused on

104 Extending quality management through the supply chain

CASE STUDY 21: QUALITY INCENTIVES SUCCESS

One of the early tasks of pick-and-place robots in car assembly was the installation of seat belt inertia reels. This appeared to be an ideal task for the robots as precise location was required and the item itself was comparatively light, well within the limits of early robots.

A major problem became obvious immediately; human assembly workers were able to orientate each component correctly prior to fitting with no additional effort or time. The robots would attempt to fit the inertia reels in whichever orientation they were provided. Where the robot was unable to fit the inertia reel due to orientation, there would be a delay to production. Where the robot was able to fit the inertia reel in an incorrect orientation, there would be no delay to production but the inertia reel seat belt wouldn't work. Repair of this fault was incredibly expensive as it involved dismantling the interior of the finished vehicle.

The immediate reaction to this problem was for customer staff to orientate the inertia reels correctly in the trays from which the robots would pick them. This substantially reduced the cost benefit of the robotic installation. The real solution was for the supplier of inertia reels to deliver them correctly orientated in the trays.

This was successfully achieved through a blend of quality premiums and penalties – a small premium was paid for each reel delivered in the correct orientation, and a large penalty imposed for each reel in an incorrect orientation, this penalty reflecting the cost of correcting the error in the assembled vehicle. This approach quickly became common in manufacturing.

---

distinct deliverables can lead to game playing by the supplier, where the supplier places maximum effort on delivering against the quality premiums at the expense of a balanced approach, leading to quality shortfalls in some areas.

Projects are usually quite risky enough, without someone trying to be clever over using quality premiums and quality penalties to boost profit, as shown in Case study 22.

7.9 Conclusions of chapter

Forming strong partnerships down supply chains, based on sound total quality management principles, helps to ensure that projects are delivered successfully. There are a number of principles that help with this:

- Select only the right suppliers (with the right expertise), and no more.
- Place the right responsibilities with the right parties, including the customer.

CASE STUDY 22: GETTING THE INCENTIVES WRONG

In 2001, a utilities company contracted with a systems integration house to provide an integrated IT solution for marketing, sales, customer relationship management, account management and billing, one of the largest IT projects in Europe at the time.

Its objective was to create a single virtual contact centre covering all services and products, across many geographically dispersed sites. The solution would identify opportunities for cross-selling and up-selling services and products to existing customers. The project was ambitious, but not unrealistic – the software packages chosen were market-leading and the contractor was very well regarded by the client.

Business benefit from the solution was believed to be quantifiable in financial terms, which led to an incentive element of the contract. A substantial bonus could be payable to the contractor, based on achievement of business benefit measured above the agreed baseline. As this was a trusted relationship, there was little in the way of penalties for failure to deliver on the core requirements. The work to be done broke down into two clear portions:

- Work needed to meet the core requirements laid down in the contract, but without additional business benefit.
- Work that had potential for delivering additional business benefits, hence bonus.

This created an unintended conflict of interest; the bonus distracted attention away from meeting the core requirements, towards bonus-generating extra requirements.

To complicate matters, the measurement of business benefits was abandoned and replaced by estimates of financial benefits made by business unit heads. This made the value of business benefits a political decision rather than a measurable fact. The unfortunate outcome of this was that business units unwilling to declare benefits saw little effort applied to meeting their contractual requirements, whereas business units willing to declare substantial benefits saw effort piled into developing additional facilities for which bonuses were foreseen.

Sadly, chasing the bonuses at the expense of meeting the contractual requirements led to a solution not fit for purpose, a court action, and the supplier losing out financially, relationally and in reputation. This is a sorry outcome due to poor use of premiums and penalties, not to mention poor quality management by the supplier.

106 Extending quality management through the supply chain

- Create a project team that crosses organisational and commercial boundaries, forging a single project organisation focused on success.
- Plan for success from the start.
- Communicate frequently and openly between companies.
- React together to problems, not against each other.
- Act swiftly to prevent problems arising.

This chapter shows the impact on project success of supply chain quality failures, causing rework and budget overruns. It recommends exploiting the synergies possible between procurement processes and supply chain quality management to drive down risk of quality failures, with their consequent costs and delays.

It recommends considering supplier auditing, and always providing clear requirements documentation with clearly-defined acceptance criteria.

It recommends creating the best relationship with suppliers that is reasonably achievable, quite possibly through using supplier development as a quality improvement strategy.

It warns of the dangers of inappropriate use of quality incentives.

7.10 Bibliography

Cousins, P., Lamming R., Lawson, B. and Squire, B. (2008) 'Strategic Supply Management – Principles, Theories and Practice', Pearson Education, ISBN: 9780273651000

Gill, N. (2009) 'Developing Cooperative Project Client-Supplier Relationships: How much to expect from relational contracts', California Management Review 51(2) 144–169

Hellard, R.B. (1993) 'Total Quality in Construction Projects', Thomas Telford Books, London ISBN: 9780727719515

Karim, K., Marosszeky, M. and Davis, S. (2006) 'Managing Subcontractor Supply Chain for Quality in Construction', University of New South Wales, Engineering, Construction and Architectural Management, Vol 13, Issue 1, pp. 27–42

Krause, D.R., Scannell, T.V. and Calantone, R. J. (2000) 'A Structural Analysis of the Effectiveness of Buying Firms' Strategies to Improve Supplier Performance', Decision Sciences, Vol 31 (1), pp. 33–55

Rogers Commission (1986) – https://science.ksc.nasa.gov/shuttle/missions/51-l/docs/rog ers-commission/table-of-contents.html

Womack, J. P. and Jones, D. T. (2003) 'Lean Thinking: Banish Waste and Create Wealth in Your Corporation', Simon & Schuster / Free Press, ISBN: 9780743231640

Further information sources

CQI, Chartered Quality Institute. CQI also has special interest groups on Engineering and Deming, amongst others.
www.apm.org.uk
www.bis.gov.uk
www.icevirtuallibrary.com

8

QUALITY ANALYSIS TECHNIQUES

If you don't measure it, you can't manage it effectively, and measuring the wrong thing can take you in the wrong direction. Financial measures are well understood, and timeliness can similarly be measured simply. Earned value techniques have been developed to integrate the measurement of these two corners of the iron triangle.

Quality can be rather harder to measure reliably, but sound metrics of progress must be based on the proven (accepted) quality of the products delivered. Many software development projects have foundered from using 'lines of code written' as the progress metric rather than 'functionality that has passed acceptance testing', not realising that writing the code is at best half the work and debugging the rest.

This chapter introduces core concepts of measurement and quantification, and then provides an overview of a number of tools and techniques used in collecting and analysing data.

It describes the 'Five Whys' (5Ys) technique for root cause analysis to discover the underlying reasons for problems, then considers a range of techniques for dealing with human error avoidance.

It concludes by showing that, even in the project environment, continuous improvement has a key role to play in improving quality management.

Learning outcomes for the chapter

After reading this chapter, the reader should understand:

- The principles of measuring quality.
- Tools and techniques for measuring quality.
- The 5Ys technique for root cause analysis.
- The principles of continuous improvement.

8.1 Measurement and analysis: accuracy and precision

There are some important terms relating to test measurements that are important in understanding results, and specifying acceptance criteria.

Accuracy and precision are two terms that are often used interchangeably, but technically have quite different meanings. When measuring something:

The **accuracy** is the closeness of the measurements (average) to that quantity's actual (true) value.

The **precision** (reproducibility or repeatability), is the degree to which repeated measurements under the same conditions show the same result.

The difference between accuracy and precision is illustrated in Figure 8.1.

- High accuracy and high precision: the shots are tightly grouped in the centre of the target (top right box).
- High accuracy and low precision: the shots are loosely grouped around the centre of the target (bottom right box).
- Low accuracy and high precision: the shots are closely grouped but not centred on the target (top left box).
- Low accuracy and low precision: the shots are loosely grouped, not centred on the target (bottom left box).

In statistical terms, accuracy is the inverse of the difference between the mean value of the measurements and the true value. Precision is the inverse of the standard deviation of the measurements, illustrated by Figure 8.2. Sigma (σ) is the Greek symbol used to represent standard deviation.

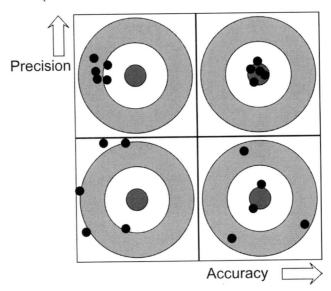

FIGURE 8.1 Difference between accuracy and precision

Quality analysis techniques **109**

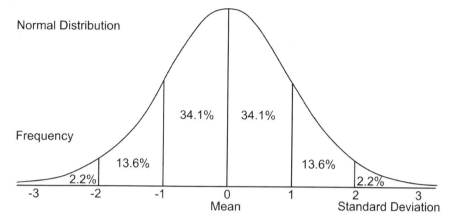

FIGURE 8.2 The normal distribution

In normal circumstances (given a 'normal distribution' of measurements), a process where the tolerance is equal to one standard deviation (1σ) will have 68 per cent of products within tolerance – the rest will be waste or scrap. Improving the process precision so that the tolerance falls at 2σ means that 95 per cent of products will be within tolerance, and only 5 per cent will be scrap. Taking this much further eventually increases precision to 6σ, where 99.99966 per cent of products are within tolerance, and scrap is negligible. The 'Six Sigma' tools and techniques take their name from this target. Figure 8.3 illustrates this.

Guidance on using statistical techniques in a quality management system is given in ISO/TR 10017:2003.

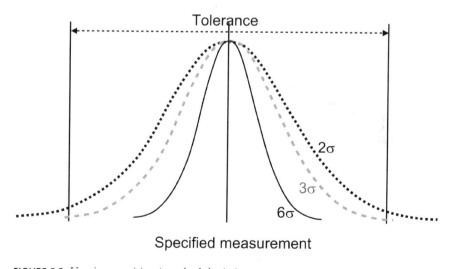

FIGURE 8.3 Varying precision/standard deviation

110 Quality analysis techniques

8.2 Quality management techniques

There are many quality management techniques available. These have been developed mainly in the manufacturing arena where consistency of large numbers of products is the desired outcome. These techniques are useful in different niches within the project management environment, but their usefulness is heavily dependent on the nature of the project. The following are the ones likely to be most relevant in a project management environment, but there is no guarantee that a technique will be useful for every project:

1. Seven Quality Tools.
2. Root cause analysis with 5Ys.
3. Prevention and mitigating actions.
4. Continuous improvement (Kaizen).
5. The Deming Cycle (PDCA).
6. Identifying wastes.
7. Process mapping.

8.2.1 Seven quality tools

The Seven Quality Tools are a simple but very effective set of techniques included in Six Sigma that can be used in quality management, problem solving, and improving processes. In this section, most of these techniques will only be referred to briefly. Some of these techniques are only effective when there are statistically significant numbers of measurements. This is only the case in certain circumstances within the project environment, limiting applicability of these tools, but they are particularly valuable during:

- Integration – analysis of test results.
- Commissioning – analysis of operational data.
- Warranty – identification of problems to be addressed under warranty.
- Service operation – detecting out of tolerance operation.
- Maintenance – early warning of degradation and incipient failure.

The seven techniques are shown in Table 8.1.

TABLE 8.1 The 7 Quality Tools

Check sheet (tally charts) Histograms Scatter diagrams	Data gathering
Control charts Flow charts	Data gathering and analysis
Cause and effect diagrams Pareto analysis	Analysis techniques

Of these, we will discuss *Pareto analysis* alone.

The Pareto principle, also known as the 80:20 rule, is named after the Italian economist who observed that 20 per cent of the population owned 80 per cent of the wealth of the nation.

Analysing the causes of problems usually reveals the 80:20 rule in action, and identifies the most significant problems or opportunities so that they can be addressed first.

An example of this was a new IT workflow system that was heavily criticised both by users and by IT Service Delivery in its post-implementation review, 3 months after go-live. Its problems were reported as 'too numerous to discuss, and too varied to analyse.' Analysis of the issue log revealed:

- 45% of logged items related to a known backup problem.
- 35% of logged items related to processes stopping without creating an alert.
- 20% were 'one-off' issues.

Operational solutions for both the significant problems were implemented within 48 hours, after which the new system was seen as reliable.

The Seven Quality Tools are useful for determining that there **is** a quality problem: having identified this fact, the next step is to understand the underlying, or root, **cause** of the problem so it can be addressed.

8.2.2 Root Cause Analysis with Five Whys

The Five Whys ('5Ys') is a very simple problem analysis technique for probing the root cause of a problem. It was developed at Toyota where it was recognised that establishing the root cause of a problem only occurred when the question 'Why?' was asked repeatedly (typically at least five times) to drill down through layers of symptoms.

5Ys requires asking questions until the root cause is reached and not accepting the answers until then. Discovering the underlying source of the problem means it can be addressed rather than the symptoms. Hunting out root causes and solving them, rather than repeating corrective actions, avoids waste. The simple example in Figure 8.4 illustrates the benefit of 5Y analysis:

The example in Figure 8.4 is simplistic, just to show the principle, and shows that repeated questioning reveals more fundamental reasons for the problem, and less superficial, so longer-lasting and more satisfactory, solutions.

In reality, the situation is usually more complex. Potentially, the questioning sequence can be taken further than just five levels of probing, to six, seven and so on until the root cause is found.

The next example, analysing the failure of a global IT programme, is an illustration of a situation where there are numerous contributory root causes, which is very common. Carrying out a 5Ys analysis resulted in a complicated 'tree' with loops and more than five levels (Figure 8.5 shows the complexity, but not the

112 Quality analysis techniques

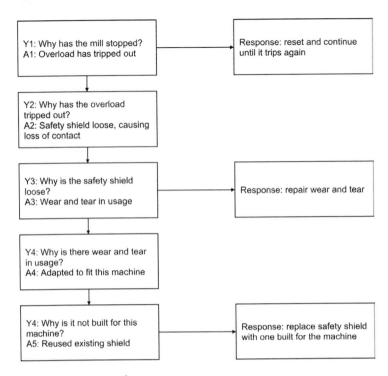

FIGURE 8.4 Basic 5Ys example

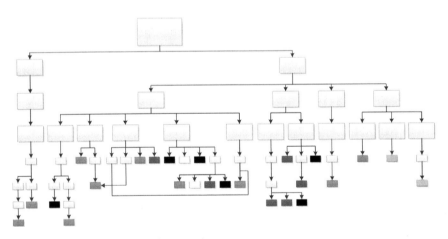

FIGURE 8.5 Topology of a real 5Ys analysis

details, which are confidential), where different lines of questioning ended up with the same root causes, causing the branches to join back up at common root causes. Lines of questioning probed management decision-making styles, IT strategy, organisational structure, relationships between IT and business users, investment

Quality analysis techniques **113**

strategy and other factors. The different grey shades code which part of the organisation was accountable for the root causes.

This branching of the analysis, resulting from alternative answers to the questions, is normal. All potential answers to the questions should be considered, as the true root cause may not be the obvious one!

8.2.3 Prevention and mitigating actions in achieving quality

When workloads and time pressures are high, it is common for people to become reactive, and for fire-fighting to prevail. When fires are frequently breaking out, all the resource can become distracted into putting them out, without considering how fires can be prevented in the first place. Corrective actions take place, but addressing the systemic issues, identifying the root causes and preventing recurrences often do not happen.

When the e-mail failed globally at a major multi-national manufacturer, it became clear that e-mail was the key management communication tool for the whole organisation, and anyone who could help was drafted away from their current workload, causing delays of several weeks on other programmes. Ironically, one of these was a new information management solution offering major benefits over e-mail. Looking into the root causes of this problem indicated the fundamental issue was the executive management didn't understand IT, with the consequences that:

- The email server update had been delayed due to cost-cutting directives.
- Ever-greater demand for mobile e-mail users overloaded the servers.
- There was no business demand for a better solution than e-mail.

The new solution would have provided a much better solution for executive management and would have off-loaded the e-mail too, but the delays to this improvement programme resulted in its eventual cancellation, leaving the dependency on e-mail unchanged.

A project cannot afford to rely on **corrective actions**; it needs to prevent problems occurring through **mitigating actions**. Preventing failures avoids the need for corrective actions. Tackling root causes and training staff in error prevention techniques prevent waste.

A simple example of failure prevention can be seen in petrol filling stations, to avoid putting the wrong fuel into a vehicle. Simple techniques are used in the nozzle design to reduce the chances of this happening, such as different sized nozzles for petrol and diesel pumps and the use of colour to alert the user to the differences, i.e. green for petrol, black for diesel. Although these techniques don't eliminate the risk altogether, they do reduce the chances of the problem occurring.

The following are common error prevention techniques, particularly effective when designed into a solution from the start:

1 Physical separation

Physically separating fireworks from a source of ignition keeps them, and any people around them, safe. Keeping fireworks in a sealed metal box when there are any sparks around means they aren't ignited accidentally.

Most of the people killed by at BP's Texas City oil refinery explosion in 2005 were attending a meeting in a hazardous area they did not need to be in. Physical separation of personnel from a potential hazard would have limited the loss of life.

2 Visual signals

Traffic lights are the most obvious use of visual signals to control safe operations (and similarly on railways).

3 Pattern recognition

An example of the pattern recognition technique is to have control panels where all the switches point up when off and down when on. This makes it obvious, even from a distance, when something is switched off/isolated. The 'glass cockpits' of modern airliners aim for 'dark and quiet' when nothing is wrong – only alerts cause warning lights to come on and alarms to sound.

4 Simple physical devices

In the workplace, a common means of separation is the use of a physical barrier or a locking system to prevent a critical piece of equipment being placed in the wrong mode, or a valve being opened in error. Physical interlocks are still common in railway signalling, as are level crossing barriers.

8.2.4 Continuous improvement (Kaizen)

Kaizen, 'good change', means continuous improvement involving everybody, i.e. team-based problem solving and generation of solutions. Continuous improvement is particularly valuable when applied to the project management processes themselves, and has lasting value in the operational and maintenance phases of the project/site.

Standards and expectations are constantly rising; so not continuously improving processes and systems is not standing still, it is going backwards. Its originator, Masaaki Imai, developed the following key guidelines for Kaizen:

1. Questioning the status quo. He argued that standards are necessary, but work rules must be changed for improvement to occur.
2. It is a management priority to develop resourcefulness in individuals and teams, and the participation of everyone in improvement activities.

Quality analysis techniques **115**

3. Identify root causes. Problems and improvement opportunities must not be solved superficially.
4. Aim to eliminate whole tasks if possible, questioning whether a task is necessary, in order to simplify processes, activities, designs and projects.

John Bicheno (2008) advocates organising continuous improvement into a hierarchy, with five distinct layers of activities, each with increasing scope, as follows:

1. Individuals seeking to improve their own work area or activities, by understanding the process in detail, why it is necessary and how it fits into wider activities.
2. Work team Kaizen to improve the team's collective work area or processes.
3. Specific improvement events which involve people in addition to the team, because the team alone cannot bring about the improvement (Kaizen Blitz events).
4. Flow Kaizen – working along a complete process. In a project environment, this could involve a review of a major process such as order placement and receipt, and would probably include process mapping to analyse in detail the 'current state' and then develop an improved process. They should be led by a project manager or the programme management office.
5. Supply Chain Kaizen involves representatives from supplier or subcontractor organisations.

Applying lower levels to a project (1–3) may be within the scope of a large project, but the higher levels need commitment from the whole organisation (4) and supply chain (5).

> *Reflective exercise: consider simple examples of how Kaizen could be used to strengthen project management in your workplace.*

8.2.5 The Deming Cycle (PDCA) of continuous improvement

The Deming Cycle, named after American quality guru W. Edwards Deming, is a key tool in continuous improvement of quality. This process can be applied to any number of situations, such as problem solving, decision making, improvement processes, etc., and works as shown in Figure 8.6.

Plan
- Define a problem or improvement opportunity.
- Gather data and analyse – identify root causes.
- Brainstorm ideas – select appropriate solution.
- Undertake cost/benefit analysis.
- Start gathering performance data as baseline.

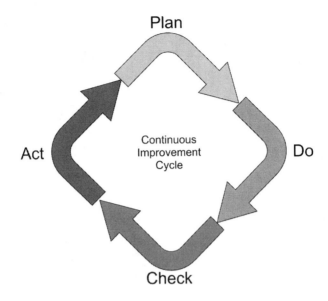

FIGURE 8.6 The Deming Cycle of continuous improvement

Do
- Testing/trials of solutions/improvements.
- Training.
- Gather improved performance data.

Check
- Analyse results of the tests/trials.
- Check effectiveness of the solution or implementation.
- Apply modifications or corrections if required.
- Learn from the mistakes using data collected.

Act
- Make the new process permanent, through new work instructions or standard operating procedures.
- Communicate the changes effectively.
- Train everyone in the new process/procedure.
- Give recognition due.
- Consider – What next?

8.2.6 Identifying wastes

As discussed in Chapter 2, waste is the only cost that can be cut without capability impacts. In the project environment, waste has an adverse impact on quality, as time, effort and money lost in waste are not delivering outputs.

Quality analysis techniques **117**

TABLE 8.2 The 7 Lean Wastes

Waste	Definition	Project office examples
Transport	Moving materials from one area to another.	Retrieving or storing files. Carrying documents to/from shared equipment, e.g. printers. Getting signatures.
Inventory	More materials or information on hand than is currently required.	Unused records in a database. Data not used. emails waiting to be read. Unprocessed paperwork.
Motion	Movement of people adds no value.	Walking to meeting rooms. Searching through manuals or catalogues. Travel between sites.
Waiting	Idle time when people, parts or information are not available when required.	Waiting for information, faxes, etc. Waiting for people, e.g. for meetings to start. Waiting for authorisations.
Over production	Generating more than the customer requires.	Giving more detail than necessary. Producing reports which are not read. Making extra copies.
Over processing	Delivering a Rolls Royce when the customer wanted a Mini.	Repeated entry or transfer of data. Printing e-mails. Printing weekly reports.
Defects	Scrap, rework, snagging.	Data entry errors. Pricing errors. Lost/missing information or specifications.

Waste may well force compromise on quality due to time, resource or financial constraints.

The **Seven Lean Wastes (mnemonic TIM WOOD)** are shown in Table 8.2, together with their definitions. Sample activities in the office environment of a project include:

Transport waste – walking to and from a printer at the opposite end of the building.
Inventory waste – store rooms full of blank forms and other stationery.
Motion waste – frequent travel between sites, rather than video conferencing.
Waiting waste – everyone waiting for the chairman before a meeting can start.

118 Quality analysis techniques

Over-production waste – issuing printed detailed reports to everyone that are not read.

Over-processing waste – entering the same information into 3 different forms.

Defects waste – printing 30 copies of a thick document, then realising there is a formatting error and having to reprint another set.

Most of these waste categories above involve losses of time and/or material.

8.2.7 Process mapping to improve efficiencies

Projects usually involve some degree of change in the way the business operates. The situation post-project will hopefully be more efficient/effective. For example, adding flue gas desulphurisation to a coal-fired power station will substantially reduce the air pollution produced, but changes the way the plant is operated, and requires the supply of the lime consumed and disposal of the gypsum produced.

Where a project is changing the way the business operates, process mapping provides a powerful but simple way to present, hence share understanding of, the way the business operates. Efficiency improvement by shortening procurement timelines is a particularly valuable aspect of project quality management, as it creates more time in which to achieve the right quality standards.

There are many different forms of process mapping tools, from brown paper charts and spaghetti diagrams, to more complex analyses, such as value stream maps. There are several books on this topic so will not be discussed further in detail, but Case study 23 shows the approach in action successfully.

CASE STUDY 23: CORE SYSTEM REPLACEMENT FOR TWO CREDIT CARD PROVIDERS

Immediately after their merger, two credit card companies wanted to replace their existing core IT system. They both had heavily customised systems, and upgrading was both painfully slow and expensive, as the customisations had to be reapplied separately to each new version.

On selecting the new IT system, a strategic decision was taken to realign the business processes in the two organisations, harmonising them both with each other, and with the functionality offered by the new system, itself a market leader. This would minimise customisation.

Central to this was creating a set of process maps that represented the target operating model, a detailed set of processes defining how the business teams would work and interact with the new solution/system, and what the system would automate. This was achieved through a series of workshops involving both companies and the software supplier.

The use of process models clearly identified:

- Where customisations had to be made for national regulatory compliance.
- Where the businesses operated differently and could harmonise going forward.
- Where harmonisation was prevented by product and market differences.

Some pragmatic customisations were allowed for key products, but the default position was to impose business process changes, rather than automatically echoing current practice. This had the potential for saving a huge amount in Through Life Costs, and reduced the software development lead-time and testing required to go live.

Both organisations migrated smoothly and successfully.

8.3 Conclusions of chapter

This chapter introduces core concepts of measurement and quantification, and a number of tools and techniques used in collecting and analysing data. It concludes that all of the techniques can be useful in the project context, but their use is situation-dependent.

The 5Ys technique for root cause analysis, discovering the underlying reasons for quality problems, is generally useful in solving recurring problems, reducing costs and delays. Repeatedly addressing symptoms, rather than identifying and fixing their root cause, is wasteful. Once the root cause is identified and its solution costed out, an informed choice can be made whether to fix the root cause or continue addressing its symptoms.

Applying techniques for avoiding human error are best applied from the start, as mistakes early in the project, when finally detected, will be both expensive and time-consuming to rectify, or even cause the complete termination of the project.

Even in the project environment, continuous improvement can play a key role in improving quality management effectiveness.

8.4 Bibliography

ISO (2003) ISO/TR 10017:2003 'Guidance on statistical techniques for ISO 9001:2000'

Further reading

'APM Body of Knowledge', 6th edition, Association for Project Management, ISBN: 9781903494400

120 Quality analysis techniques

Price, F. (2017) 'Right First Time: Using Quality Control for Profit', Routledge, ISBN: 0-7045-0522-3

Bicheno, J. (2008) 'The Lean Toolbox: The Essential Guide to Lean Transformation', Picsie Books, ISBN: 9780954124410

Quality Management Systems – www.dti.gov.uk/quality/qms

Tools and Techniques for Process Improvement – www.dti.gov.uk/quality/tools

9

PROJECT MANAGEMENT TECHNIQUES VITAL TO QUALITY

Correctly using some standard project management techniques is important to project quality management success. Quality management isn't independent from the normal running of a project, but a core concern to be balanced with schedule and budget.

This chapter reviews the core project management techniques that are vital for delivering a quality outcome, the management of:

- Requirements.
- Change and configuration.
- Risk.
- Project performance.
- Knowledge.

As these are disciplines already entrenched deeply in project management, their balanced focus on quality should incur little or no increase in cost or time, boosting quality management for free.

Learning outcomes for the chapter

On completing this chapter, the reader will understand:

- The relationship between quality and requirements management.
- The relationship between quality and change management.
- The relationship between quality and risk management.
- The need to balance quality measures with cost and schedule in project performance management.
- The relationship between quality and knowledge management.

122 Project management techniques vital to quality

9.1 Requirements management

Given that a primary definition of quality is 'conformance to requirements', effective requirements management is essential for projects to achieve quality, hence success.

9.1.1 What are requirements?

Requirements are 'a statement of the need a project has to satisfy' according to the APM BoK (APM, 2012).

Requirements come in a wide range of types, only some of which are functional but all of which need to be satisfied.

1 True requirements and documented requirements

True/real/genuine requirements are those attributes of a solution that will make it fit for purpose. They exist as concepts, and may or may not be recognised and accurately documented. They can extend far beyond the technological focus of the project, and will include any human factors in the use of the solution.

Identification of all **true/real/genuine requirements** can be extremely challenging, as there is a tendency within a project to break down the problem into pieces, then focus on some of them, especially the technical elements, to the exclusion of others (especially the human factors) in creating the solution. Systems Thinking helps in exploring the whole scope of the requirements and the (potentially complex) interactions between elements of the solution, technical and human.

Requirements also include the need to comply with any legal and regulatory constraints on a solution. These constraints themselves may be couched as compliance with particular published standards, such as pressure testing standards for steam vessels and piping, nuclear testing standards for handling radioactive material, aviation standards for aircraft production, and the General Data Protection Regulations for computer systems.

Documented requirements are the attempted representations (usually textual and diagrammatic) of the true requirements, and are often referred to simply as 'the requirements'. The documented requirements may differ from the true requirements in a number of ways:

- Being incomplete.
- Being incorrect.
- Being incoherent (internal contradictions).
- Specifying a solution (possibly inappropriate), rather than explaining the true requirements.

Since documented requirements are normally the basis of contracts, any of the above problems may lead to contractual issues and project variations/change notes, causing delays and cost escalation.

2 Functional requirements and non-functional requirements

Requirements fall into two categories:

- What the solution should do (functional requirements).
- Everything else (non-functional requirements).

Functional requirements are the natural focus of customer attention in projects, as they define how the customers and solution users will operate once the solution is delivered.

Non-functional requirements are prone to being under-defined or even over-looked unless the project organisation is highly disciplined and professional. Key non-functional requirements to be considered include:

- Initial solution performance, and capacity for growth.
- Usability, and training requirements for users.
- Availability, reliability and maintainability (ARM).
- Security (both physical and cyber).
- Adaptability/scalability/longevity.

3 Specifications

Specifications define the solution and its components. Whereas requirements **drive** the design process, the specifications result **from** the design process, to describe the solution. The terms 'specifications' and 'requirements' tend to be used inter-changeably, but this confuses the situation. Sometimes the requirements include specifications. If this is the case, should the specified item be unfit for purpose, accountability for failure lies solely with the customer.

9.1.2 Requirement importance/prioritisation

Not all requirements **must** be met; the importance of each requirement should be captured. The design process needs to trade off meeting requirements against cost and time – this requires confidence by the design team in being able to drop low-importance requirements to achieve project success.

Typically, requirements are classed as one of:

- Mandatory/essential – MUST be satisfied.
- Highly desirable – SHOULD be satisfied, but can be sacrificed under pressure.
- Nice-to-have – COULD be satisfied; not essential at all, but would be beneficial.
- WILL NOT have – to be excluded from the proposed solution.

This classification system is frequently known as MoSCoW (APM, 2012). Arriving at this classification is usually a qualitative process, as quantifying the benefits of

124 Project management techniques vital to quality

individual requirements is difficult and time-consuming. Critical peer review of requirement priority is important, as requirement owners may have difficulty assigning lower priorities than MUST.

9.1.3 Requirements capture/definition

The first stage in requirements management, and usually the most difficult, is known as requirements capture, or requirements definition. The following three points are important foundations for understanding the true/real/genuine requirements, so being able to understand and document them.

1 Critical Success Criteria – what will make the project a success/failure?

True requirements can be revealed by asking probing questions about the critical success criteria of the project, and what success looks like. This system level thinking causes customers to take a step back from 'specifying' mode into a holistic reflective mode. These high-level criteria give a good insight to what is really important.

2 Planning for acceptance from the start

Planning for acceptance, if left until late in the project, can draw in many stakeholders who have often not been consulted effectively previously. This results in a flurry of last-minute changes as their insights and consequent changes are taken on-board, with consequent delay and cost escalation. Planning for acceptance from the start stimulates 'Big Picture' (Systems) thinking, encouraging the stakeholders to consider scenarios that may well be overlooked in the documented requirements otherwise.

3 The role of the user in ensuring usability

An unusable solution is worthless. It is easy for designers and engineers to create an unusable solution that meets the functional requirements but is still not fit for purpose. One such instance we encountered was a web-based order form for a contact centre that lengthened call duration by 200 per cent; naturally, it was never used.

Involving users in the capture and validation of requirements is very important. This minimises the late changes which result from engaging users only in acceptance testing of the solution. This is a significant factor in the popularity of Agile methodologies.

9.1.4 Requirements validation – project lifecycle choice

The point in the project lifecycle that the documented requirements are validated i.e. are proven to be a correct representation of the business needs, influences the project approach needed.

1 Waterfall

Waterfall methods apply a linear, logical and structured approach to the development and delivery of complicated solutions. Reverse flows are not catered for; this approach assumes that uncertainty is addressed fully at each stage. The principal weakness of pure waterfall lifecycles/methodologies is that the documented requirements are only fully validated, i.e. are demonstrated to meet fully the needs and expectations of the customer, at the end of the project, when the completed solution undergoes acceptance testing to verify it meets the requirements. Any significant flaws in the documented requirements revealed at this stage virtually guarantees the project will finish late and over-budget. Waterfall is the best choice when the requirements are clear, and incremental development isn't possible.

2 Agile

'Agile' methods are incremental, iterative methods that use successive time-limited development periods to explore the requirements and move the solution functionality onwards. Agile methods address validation of requirements continuously through the close-knit integration of the customers/users into the project team. However, there is a risk that using an Agile methodology could result in going down technical blind-alleys, and consequent rework. Agile is only viable where incremental development can occur, and is powerful in developing a validated set of requirements.

9.1.5 Requirements verification and project acceptance

Formal acceptance of the solution, hence project success, needs verification that the requirements have been met.

Complicated solutions require complicated testing, but the combinatorial explosion of all cases needed to test a complicated solution exhaustively makes it prohibitively expensive and time-consuming, if not impossible.

This can only be addressed by quality assurance – design for prevention of defects rather than relying on their detection afterwards – coupled with carefully-designed testing to allow acceptance.

Having explained that requirements management is the foundation of delivering quality, it is clear that all parties need to be working to a consistent definition of the requirements. As requirements are almost guaranteed to change during the project lifecycle, the next key project management discipline vital to delivering quality is change control.

9.2 Change control

Nothing stays the same for long – the longer the project, the more things change. The APM BoK (APM, 2012) defines change control as:

126 Project management techniques vital to quality

> *'...the process that ensures that all changes made to a project's baselined scope, time, cost and quality objectives or agreed benefits are identified, evaluated, approved, rejected or deferred.'*

People working to out-of-date information create problems that can cause the whole project to fail. Change management and control minimises this.

Managing customers' expectations is closely linked to change management. A project is a success when the stakeholders are satisfied. This means that stakeholders:

- Have got what they were expecting (or more).
- For what they were expecting to pay (or less).
- When they were expecting it (or earlier).

Elements of time, cost and quality in the project are inter-related:

- When the deadline is required to be earlier than anticipated, customer expectation must be modified to include changes in cost and quality/scope.
- When extra requirements are introduced during the project, customer expectation and contracts must be modified to include changes in time, cost and other areas of quality.

Changes within a project can include any of the following:

- Unavoidable (e.g. a supplier goes out of business).
- Highly desirable (opportunity arises to improve the benefit substantially).
- Unnecessary (the perceived benefit improvements are not significant).
- Undesirable (supplier seeking to save costs, cut corners, change their process to fit with other customer requirements etc).

An effective change control system needs the following features:

1. Formal control of any proposed changes to the project.
2. Impact assessment by all relevant stakeholders and project sponsor.
3. Definite and timely decisions.
4. Clear delegated authority for change decisions.
5. Ability to assess changes actioned without approval retrospectively to evaluate all impacts and ensure they are dealt with.

Change management **discipline** is essential to avoid discrepancies between documentation and expectations. This is helped by a simple, transparent control process (consistent with the APM BoK (2012), shown in Figure 9.1.

> *Reflective exercise: is change control seen as a positive feature or a tedious chore to be avoided in your environment? Why is that?*

Project management techniques vital to quality **127**

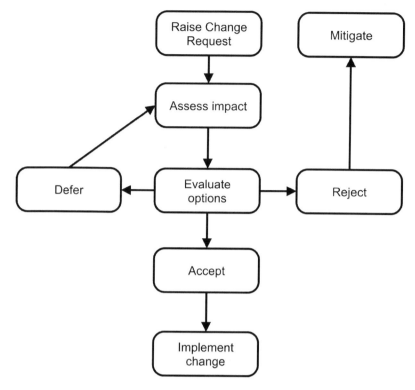

FIGURE 9.1 Typical change control process

9.3 Risk management in project quality

A project risk is an uncertain event or condition that, were it to occur, would have a positive or negative effect on a project's objective (APM, 2012). Quality-related risks include:

- The project failing to realise the benefits in the business case.
- The project creating products that are not fit for purpose or non-compliant.
- Unmanaged changes to the requirements during the project.
- Changes in legal and regulatory standards, redefining success.
- Changes in client management, affecting project priority and stakeholders.
- Changes in suppliers (for example, suppliers go out of business or are taken over), threatening timely delivery of quality.

9.3.1 Applying risk management

Risk management is a process that allows individual risk events and overall risk to be understood and managed proactively, optimising success by minimising threats and maximising opportunities. (APM, 2012)

128   Project management techniques vital to quality

Risk management aims to do at least one of:

- make risks less likely to happen.
- make the impact of risks less severe if they happen.
- make contingency plans, and know exactly what to do if risks happen.

Together these three reasons make risk management effectiveness a leading indicator of project management excellence.

Case study 24 describes a failure in quality risk management.

In contrast, getting quality risk management right can be hugely satisfying, as Case study 25 shows.

CASE STUDY 24: QUALITY RISK MANAGEMENT – GETTING IT WRONG

During the telecoms billing project described in Case study 1, there was one failure in risk management. Executive pressure induced the project manager to carry out the final project phase without the comprehensive level of testing applied previously, and without the proven means of reversing the transfer should it go wrong. This was done in order to reduce the duration of the project by one month. However, this approach introduced the risk of errors with a significant probability of occurrence and without firm contingency plans in place.

Mitigation consisted of two pilots carried out earlier in the project. After the pilots, the risk was assessed as low and the difficulty of resolving any errors seen as tolerable. Unfortunately, neither of the two pilots had revealed a fundamental flaw in the team's understanding of what was necessary for a successful migration of services, and the project had its only failure at the end of the long run of successes.

There was significant customer impact; understanding what had gone wrong was time-consuming and building a mechanism to repair it took even longer. Trying to avoid a one-month extension created three months of grief for project and customers alike.

CASE STUDY 25: QUALITY RISK MANAGEMENT – GETTING IT RIGHT

A project to host and relaunch a public service website included a contractual requirement for the data centres to be connected to the customer's secure network.

The network partner's service level agreement (SLA) for installing a new connection was 60 days. At the start of the project this was not seen as too threatening, however it was logged as a risk and tracked, In the course of the project, various delays resulted in the order being placed well after the original planned date.

At this point, it become clear that the SLA referred to working days not calendar days, so the probability that the connection would not be delivered in time grew substantially. This risk was then managed actively. Due to its severe potential impact, delaying when the website could go live, this risk received a high priority, and a suitable contingency plan was investigated and approved. Further investigation revealed the contingency plan would cost only £5000, and soon after the development of the contingency solution was triggered.

The day before the connection was due to go live, the network partner announced a forecast delay of two months due to a supply chain mix-up; work had not even started. The project team already had the contingency solution approved, developed and tested. What could have been disastrous to the project became a source of mild relief that the investment on the contingency solution was justified. The contingency plan was put into action and the project delivered on time.

Guidance on effective management of quality risks, consistent with the APM BoK and PRINCE2, follows.

1 Plan for risks from the start

Rigorous risk assessment and management has greatest impact during the early project period, like all quality management activities. Early project risk planning allows the estimation of schedule contingency and budget contingency before full commitment to delivery.

However, risk management is an iterative process. It offers maximum overall benefit when applied throughout the project lifecycle. This can be difficult to sustain because, done well, it is routine and unexciting – putting out fires is much more exciting than preventing them.

The frequency of risk reviews depends on the circumstances of the project, running in practice as often as daily in the final deadline approaches.

2 Set up risk management

The basic process is illustrated in Figure 9.2, consistent with the APM 'Project Risk Assessment and Management' method.

Step 1: Identification of risks – What **could** go wrong? (If it's **already gone wrong** it's an **issue**)

- Explore possible risks. Two very useful techniques are:

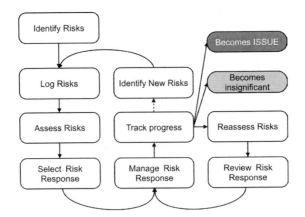

FIGURE 9.2 Risk management process

- Search the risk logs and the lessons learned logs of similar projects.
- Every time an issue occurs within a project, add the risk that it will happen again. Preventing the recurrence of issues is much easier as everyone has 20:20 hindsight.

• Establish a risk management process:
  • Logging, reviewing, planning for and reporting risk upwards to manage expectations.
  • Encourage 'no blame' openness, assigning responsibility for managing each risk.
  • Repeating risk identification/assessment exercises frequently so risk management stays fresh.

• Build the **RAID** Register to manage **R**isks, and include **A**ssumptions, **I**ssues and **D**ependencies.

Step 2: Risk Assessment – Understand each risk event's impact (consequences). The main things to assess are:

- Impact and severity.
- Probability.

Ideally, the scores are based on **objective** definitions.
   Step 3: Risk response
   Strategies for dealing with each risk include one or more of:

- Mitigating risk – reducing the likelihood of it happening, and/or reducing the impact if it does happen. Mitigation has a cost, and a lead time to implement that drives the risk's **urgency**.

Project management techniques vital to quality **131**

- Transferring risk – passing the risk to another party, usually with a cost (e.g. insurance premium).
- Avoiding risk – changing the project to skirt round the risk.
- Sharing risk – usually with the supply chain.
- Retaining risk – decide to accept the risk for now – 'wait and see'.
- Setting up contingency time buffers and budgets – allowance to recover from risks becoming issues.

The right responses depend on the specific quality risk, and include:

- Clarify requirements.
- Select different supplier.
- Share risk with supplier.
- Change design.
- Plan for pilot phase.
- Schedule earlier testing.
- Engage third party inspection.
- Schedule more time for integration.

This leads to understanding, for each risk:

- **Urgency** – lead-time to when action is needed.
- **Priority**, calculated from factors including severity, probability and urgency to rank where efforts should be focussed **at the moment**.

Step 4: Manage risk response
Responses may include:

- Design changes.
- Contract variations.
- New contracts with third parties.
- Engaging extra inspectors.
- Extra test plans.
- Project plan – add time for risk.
- Project budget – add funds for risk.
- Risk monitoring and control (through priority-driven regular risk management reviews).
- Contingency planning – creating plans that will be used if a risk occurs i.e. to handle fallout when it happens.

Contingency planning isn't easy for most people, so there is often a pressure to leave it out, and deal with any problems through fire-fighting. However, not having a contingency plan has consequences that can be severe:

132 Project management techniques vital to quality

- Slower managerial response, as analysis and decision takes time.
- Risk of mistakes made under pressure, even making things worse.

3 Controlling risk during the project

To minimise unplanned deviations, risks need to be managed actively throughout the project, frequently monitoring progress against the current top priority risks. Risk management needs to be dynamic:

- Controlling mitigation plans (mitigation is reducing the probability, severity or both, of the risk **before** it occurs).
- Controlling contingency plans (contingency plans are implemented **after** the risk occurs, becoming an issue), setting and reviewing their trigger points.

Ideally, maintaining the RAID log and project plan are coupled; mitigation and contingency activities need reflecting in the project plan after each risk review:

- Taking positive action to prevent/overcome deviations from plan.
- Assigning risk responses to those best qualified to mitigate or plan contingencies.

If risk management has been effective, when something goes wrong the impact has already been minimised and contingency plans will be ready to roll immediately.

The following three case studies (26, 27 and 28) demonstrate the tangible benefits of active risk management.

CASE STUDY 26: RISK MITIGATION

A new IT system was being developed (a business intelligence facility on a corporate data warehouse) to replace a much more limited capability on Windows PCs and server. The budget for this project was in excess of £1 million.

When reviewing the test plan, the portfolio manager noticed that no testing of the interactive performance had been planned (a non-functional requirement that had been overlooked). The risk was raised that the users could possibly experience slower response times from the multi-million pound data warehouse than from their cheap PCs. Such a slowing would reduce productivity and would lead to complaints and dissatisfaction. Interactive performance testing was the obvious mitigation action, and this revealed that in certain circumstances the new system was slower. Minor redesign of the facility led to significant performance improvements and the new solution always responding faster than the PCs it replaced. This, coupled with additional functionality, meant user satisfaction with the new solution was high.

Project management techniques vital to quality **133**

CASE STUDY 27: RISK MITIGATION

A railway engineering company earned all its revenue through railway infra-structure projects. These projects depended on weekend 'possessions' of the railway to do the work. Their top problem was recurrent issues; the same mis-takes and problems were arising week after week. The project managers were so busy fire-fighting the fallout from these issues that they didn't address the underlying problems. Introducing rigorous risk management forced them to develop mitigation plans. Within four weeks, the level of recurrent issues had dropped by 25 per cent, freeing up the project managers' time to make further improvements.

CASE STUDY 28: RISK CONTINGENCY

Multiple projects can affect the same business systems at the same time. These interdependencies must be managed between the projects involved. In one instance, a project that was transferring customers to a different system was expected to wait for the successful completion of a major upgrade to the target system. This was incorporated into the project plan.

Unfortunately, the system upgrade, already substantially delayed, contin-ued to slip. Mitigation plans were investigated, including lending resources to the upgrade project, but it was decided the only viable contingency plan was to start transferring customers before the upgrade. This would add effort and complexity to the project hence increase costs, but would prevent slippage while maintaining quality. Invoking the contingency plan avoided a six-month delay and the adverse quality impacts that pressure to recover that delay would have caused, while still remaining within budget.

9.3.2 Risk management tools

Many projects regard risk management as being simple enough to manage either with spreadsheets or even Word documents. This is true for simple projects, but particularly in large engineering or construction projects, the scale of the risk man-agement task is great (with so many products that need quality assurance) and effective risk management really benefits from a good IT solution.

There are many commercial software packages available for managing risk; most of these focus on financial or Enterprise-wide risk management, but some address the project environment.

134 Project management techniques vital to quality

TABLE 9.1 A Basic Risk Log Template

Description:	Impact:	Severity:		Owner:
		Probability:		
		Urgency:		
When raised:	Target date:	Comments:		
Mitigation tasks:	Owner:	Target date:	Progress	
Contingency tasks:	Owner:	When:		

Reflective exercise: pick a quality risk from your own experience; complete the risk log template (Table 9.1).

Reflective exercise: 'Risk Management is a project management activity, not a quality management activity, so doesn't belong in a book on quality management' – list as many points for (at least 3) and against (at least 3) this statement as you can. Do you agree or disagree with the statement?

9.4 Measuring project performance in delivering quality

A project's performance needs to be measured in order to confirm progress against plan and to track its efficiency and effectiveness.

Key Performance Indicators (KPIs) are measures, both financial and non-financial, used to **quantify** performance and for a project need to be **tied to the project's targets**.

9.4.1 Effectiveness versus efficiency – only one is vital

ISO 9000 defines:

Effectiveness – the extent to which planned activities are realised and planned results achieved.

Efficiency – the relationship between the result achieved and the resources used.

Figure 9.3 shows how effectiveness measures achieving objectives, efficiency the use of resources.

In manufacturing and most process environments, the focus leans heavily towards **efficiency**.

In the project environment, the priority must be **effectiveness**. If a project isn't effective in meeting its objectives, there is no point in being efficient.

9.4.2 How can you manage performance if you don't measure it?

In today's fast-moving world, business change never stops – it has become continuous as organisations struggle to survive. Challenging timescales have become the norm; changes rarely complete before the next change starts and in the worst case, requirements change faster than they can be delivered.

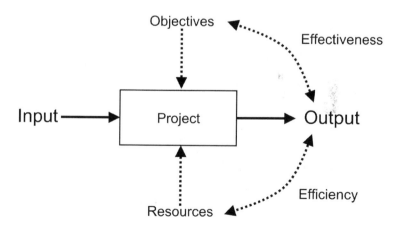

FIGURE 9.3 Efficiency versus effectiveness in the project context

136 Project management techniques vital to quality

Monitoring project quality performance allows forecasting of whether targets will be met. This requires careful selection of what to monitor, making sure the right thing is measured.

9.4.3 Challenges in selecting the right quality KPIs

Selecting the correct set of metrics (things to measure) is vital – good metrics will allow performance shortfalls and failures to be identified promptly and dealt with. Poorly-chosen metrics will at best hide the truth, and at worst give completely misleading answers. It is important to select metrics that give the right balance between time, cost and quality for each project.

> *Reflective exercise: what are suitable quality KPIs in your area of work, and the issues with collecting the right data?*

The main project KPIs (and how you want them to change) are usually fairly obvious e.g.:

- Milestones achieved by their planned date (up).
- Acceptance rates (up).
- Cost overrun against budget (down).
- Defects (down).

Managing performance requires changing project and operational activities and priorities so the KPIs move in the right direction. There are substantial challenges to making this happen, some of these include:

1. The KPIs needed to drive performance are not always obvious.
2. It takes time and effort to measure performance; timesheets are particularly tedious to complete accurately, so there is a temptation not to bother.
3. Separation between departments leads to fragmentation of knowledge.
4. Efficiency is focused on, at the expense of effectiveness.
5. People 'game play' to maximise their KPI 'score'.
6. Over-simplistic KPIs conceal the true problem.

Table 9.2 makes some recommendations for solving these challenges.

The benefits of setting and measuring the right KPIs can be enormous, as Case study 29 shows.

Project management techniques vital to quality **137**

TABLE 9.2 Challenges to measuring project performance

Challenge	Recommendation
Selecting and delivering the right KPIs.	Work from first principles, not what everyone else uses, then have the candidate KPIs reviewed independently. Use IT in calculating complex KPIs. Check KPIs against standard maturity models to make sure nothing has been missed.
Time taken for measurement.	Reduce effort through automation.
Competition between units leading to compartmentalisation of knowledge.	Increased organisational flexibility and mobility helps, objectives need to be set that minimise this.
Efficiency at the expense of innovation	Reward innovation as well as efficiency
Game Playing to maximise 'score'.	The 'score' must measure what you really want!

CASE STUDY 29: FINANCIAL SERVICES COMPLIANCE PROJECT

A high street bank had to prove itself compliant with new regulations before the deadline, and faced loss of its licenses to sell mortgages and general insurance unless it could. A new IT system had been commissioned, and a new sales process designed to achieve compliance. All that was needed was to train the staff.

For Phase 1, the staff were trained by the training department, who reported progress to the project team. Unfortunately, extrapolating from their progress reports suggested they would miss the target by 2–4 weeks, as shown in Figure 9.4.

A discussion with the Training Department revealed they had no plans against which progress could be tracked, and hadn't appreciated they would probably deliver late. They put in place immediate actions to increase their training rate, created and shared a plan and the project was a resounding success.

Phase 2 was to be trained out through the branch and contact centre staff themselves, and no progress tracking capability existed at all. A completely new progress reporting system was designed, built and deployed using existing facilities (paper forms, fax, Excel and e-mail) in just two weeks to repeat the success of phase 1.

138 Project management techniques vital to quality

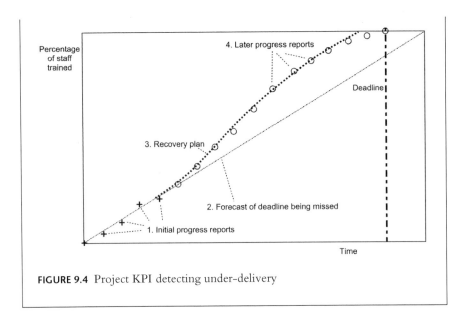

FIGURE 9.4 Project KPI detecting under-delivery

9.5 Capturing, managing and sharing knowledge

Knowledge is power ('*Scientia potentia est*', Sir Francis Bacon) as it allows the right decisions to be made, and the right actions carried out.

9.5.1 What is knowledge management?

'Knowledge management (KM) is getting the right information to the right people at the right time, helping people create knowledge and share it, and acting upon information in ways that will measurably improve the performance of the project, organisation and its partners.'

NASA Office of the Chief Knowledge Officer (NASA, Online)

According to NASA (Online), the primary benefit is that people can access the information they need more easily, supporting better decisions, so work more effectively. KM helps in:

- Disseminating knowledge between projects and involved parties to boost consistently high levels of shared understanding.
- Helping people organise and share existing knowledge, to enrich each other's understanding.
- Facilitating collaboration through working with shared knowledge.

Effective knowledge sharing and communication binds the project together, but is the first thing to suffer when the pressure is on. It is also the most important thing to maintain when the pressure is on!

Project management techniques vital to quality **139**

> *Reflective exercise: Look back on a recent project and consider the following questions.*
>
> - *When couldn't you find the right information?*
> - *When was information out-of-date?*
> - *When did information get lost or forgotten?*
> - *When was it unclear what you were being asked to do?*

Effective communication underpins much of a team's success – knowledge management is about achieving that.

> *Reflective exercise: do you work as a team:*
>
> - *In your immediate circle?*
> - *In projects?*
> - *With other departments outside the project?*
> - *With suppliers?*

The following IT tools all help manage knowledge and are useful in building team working and increasing team effectiveness.

9.5.2 KM tools: workflow management systems

A workflow management system is an IT system that automatically progresses work between people to produce the final output(s).

It may support many different workflows, each tailored to a specific task. For example, in a project, a change request would be routed from the initiator to the project office for logging and then to the change board for impact assessment and approval.

The system passes work to the individual or group responsible for each step in sequence; once the step is complete (the software can automate some of the checking), the work is passed to the people responsible for the next step.

Uncompleted/overdue tasks are flagged for follow-up.

Workflow management systems may control automated processes in addition to replacing paper transfers. If, for example, the above change request document is created is a Word template but must be loaded into the change log database, an automated process could move the text from the document into the database, before putting the change into the impact assessment process.

The process and information flow model will often be unique to the organisation (or to the project if it is distinctive enough); building the model and configuring the

140 Project management techniques vital to quality

system is a significant piece of work, usually requiring specialist consultancy, but once configured, maintenance can usually be carried out in-house. The value of workflow management systems for project administrative actions is obvious:

- The effort required in administration is reduced.
- Tracking and performance management of administrative processes is automated.
- Work no longer gets lost in someone's in tray.

9.5.3 Lesson learned logs and quality plans

'Only a fool learns [only] from his own mistakes. The wise man learns from the mistakes of others' (attributed to Otto Bismarck) is a good motto for project managers. Learning from the past is important to getting things right in the future.

Recording 'Lessons [to be] learned' is easy, but there is no point if no one is going to read it. A 'Lessons Learned' report on its own is worthless – it is the improvement activities it stimulates that deliver the value. The obvious targets are the people working on similar activities within this, or other, projects. Hard-won lessons need to be shared with, and by, others (becoming 'legendary') so that others can learn. The true quality-related targets for lessons learned is future quality planning. Face-to-face interaction is needed to drive home the lessons learned. Actions are needed to embed the lesson, be it changes to designs, processes, standards, templates, standard operating procedures (SOPs), tooling etc.

9.5.4 Filing and publication of knowledge and information

The key objectives of filing and publication are to make information and documentation:

- Easy to find.
- Easy to access.
- Easy to update (under strict controls).
- Always current.

Microsoft's SharePoint is a commonly used tool for filing and publication of information as it is part of their Office Suite. It is designed to meet enterprise knowledge management requirements. Microsoft claims SharePoint allows for creating and managing a wide spectrum of features such as intranet portals, extranet portals, websites, document and file management, and workflow automation.

There are numerous web-based alternatives with widely varying approaches, functionality and costs.

Enterprise content and document management helps to manage 'unstructured data' such as electronic documents or scanned images of paper documents, including different versions and change histories. In addition to providing digital record management systems compliant with quality standards, these systems also de-duplicate documents, which can substantially reduce data storage, and cut the carbon footprint of IT.

Engineering data management systems (EDMSs) are a specialist type of content and document management system designed to handle the files produced by computer aided design (CAD) systems and are often offered by CAD system vendors. EDMSs offer functionality that has largely converged with enterprise content and document management, while retaining the specialist focus on CAD drawings.

They need to provide automatic versioning of files/documents/drawings, version control (including notification that a document has been updated) and approval. They are designed to facilitate collaborative working with the aim of reducing total lead-time to delivery.

Microsoft explains that an *intranet portal* simplifies and standardises access to enterprise information and applications on a corporate network. It helps a company manage its data, applications, and information more easily, while increasing employee engagement, centralising process management, reducing new staff training costs, and providing tacit knowledge capture. Using an Intranet portal has important strengths:

- Standard operating procedures can be kept up to date and instantly accessible.
- No need to deploy a wide range of software to all desktops.
- Many tools e.g. Microsoft Office, have HTML or PDF export capabilities making it easy to maintain content.
- Hypertext links makes it easy to navigate to information.
- Search tools, like the Internet, can be provided for intranets.

Extranet sites can provide secure web access to project participants outside the secure IT perimeter of an organisation. This is especially important in supply chains e.g. e-Sourcing or regulated processes. e-Sourcing solutions can have significant benefits for supply chain quality management as they support rigorous application of standards across a virtual team that is multi-site, multi-discipline and multi-party, using:

- Workflow automation and tracking.
- Communications.
- All parties integrated into single process consistent with quality standards and processes.
- Increased compliance with corporate and government standards and regulations.

9.5.5 Distillation of data into insight

Few people want to access lots of raw data or documents; they want the insight as to what it all means so they can plan their response. The process of turning

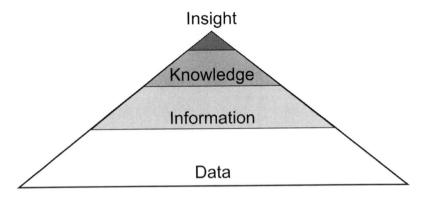

FIGURE 9.5 Distilling insight from data

data into insight is its 'distillation', reducing volume and concentrating knowledge content – see Figure 9.5.

There is no particular standard as to who carries out distillation (although PMO staff are usually heavily involved for routine tasks) or how it should be done (progress reporting is a classic distillation exercise). There is a wide selection of tools to support it, however. The important thing is that it is **done**. Without this analysis and distillation, the project and its parent organisation will accumulate progressively more data, documents and information and people will be able to access it, but won't be able to find what they need.

Case study 30 shows the dramatic benefits of data distillation in performance management.

CASE STUDY 30: PROFITABILITY IN INSURANCE

A long-established insurance broker had been acquired by a US venture capitalist due to its steadily declining profitability. The broker applied a standard mark-up to its products and collected costs against its operations, a commercial approach that had worked successfully for centuries.

Faced with declining profits and new owners, they had to do something very different. They launched a programme that, starting with the unit handling the highest value products, collected costs against the products they were selling, to measure product profitability.

The results amazed them – nearly half the products this unit was selling were loss-making due to their associated costs, despite the generous mark-up. The insight into what made a product profitable allowed them to revise their product range and pricing, reversing the decline in profits.

9.6 Conclusions of chapter

This chapter concludes that correctly applying standard project management disciplines to ensuring quality is delivered can deliver substantial benefits with little overhead.

Requirements management is the most obvious, as quality is defined as 'conformance to requirements'.

Change control (and configuration management) are essential to providing the right product to the right specification.

Risk management, when used proactively, addresses the causes of poor quality on a case-by-case basis to boost the delivery of quality products.

Performance management is a key tool in identifying potential for slippage and quality problems before they become serious issues, allowing preventative measures to be applied early.

Knowledge management is vital for delivering a quality outcome as that knowledge is needed to accurately and reliably define what is needed.

As these disciplines are already certain to be in place, they can deliver a substantial quality benefit at negligible additional cost or resource requirement.

All of these benefit from clear process design, rigorous application and appropriate IT support.

9.7 Bibliography

APM (2012) 'APM Body of Knowledge', 6th edition, Association for Project Management, ISBN: 9781903494400

BSI (2015) 'BS EN ISO 9000:2015 Quality management systems, Fundamentals and Vocabulary', British Standards Institution, ISBN: 9780580788789

NASA (online), NASA Office of the Chief Knowledge Officer – https://km.nasa.gov/what-is-km/

Nicholson, J. (1982) 'How do you Manage?' BBC Books, ISBN: 0 563 36311 8/5

Further reading – requirements

Alexander, I. and Stevens, R. (2002) 'Writing Better Requirements', Addison-Wesley, Boston

Robertson, S. and Robertson, J. (2004) 'Requirements-led Project Management: Discovering David's Slingshot', Addison-Wesley, Boston

10

IT PROJECT QUALITY MANAGEMENT

IT projects have some particular challenges in delivering quality, due to the levels of ambiguity and uncertainty that often surround their requirements, and a lack of customer understanding of how IT works and what it can offer. This makes it even more important to strike the right balance between quality, schedule and budget.

Cost or time pressures can lead to skimping on understanding the requirements. As these are often complex for IT projects, the resulting solution may be faced with rework to fulfil requirements emerging during acceptance testing.

This chapter looks at how different methodologies address these challenges, and compares their strengths and weaknesses. It explains the particular importance of the user interface in successful solutions, and how to ensure this is addressed, from design to training.

Non-functional requirements, often overlooked, are explored, as are special requirements for safety-critical and control systems.

The testing and acceptance of IT solutions are covered, verifying the requirements have been met, that the solution is fit for purpose and meets the business requirements.

This chapter focuses on areas that are particularly challenging in IT projects delivering a solution that is fit for purpose. These are:

1. Requirements management.
2. User interface design.
3. Training users.
4. Performance and other non-functional requirements.
5. Safety-critical and controls systems.
6. Testing and acceptance.

IT project quality management **145**

Learning outcomes for the chapter

On completing this chapter, the reader will understand:

- The importance and challenges of requirements management in IT projects.
- The development of Agile methods to address requirements challenges.
- The importance of engaging the end user throughout the project, from requirements definition to training.
- Test phases in typical IT projects.

10.1 Requirements: the challenge of understanding the goal

Requirements management for IT projects often involves a high level of ambiguity or uncertainty. The rapid pace of IT evolution creates challenges, and has driven requirements management techniques forward.

The APM BoK (APM, 2012) refers to structured methodologies for the development of IT solutions, giving as examples the structured systems analysis and design method (SSADM) for 'Waterfall', and the dynamic systems development method (DSDM) for 'Agile'.

10.1.1 Waterfall structured methods

'Waterfall' describes sequential methods developed in the 70s and 80s to replace the anarchy of unstructured development. Early computer applications were comparatively simple, automating repetitive Data Processing activities. Early computer scientists were true 'boffins', very intelligent and able to hold the complete design in their heads.

As the scope of computer usage expanded, two factors demanded change; computer programs became steadily more complicated, and more and more programmers were merely ingenious rather than geniuses.

Waterfall methods apply a linear, logical and structured set of tools that help with development and delivery of complicated solutions. There are various ways of presenting the waterfall approach, but one graphical representation, the 'V Model' of solution design and development (see Figure 10.1) takes the linear flow and adds a second dimension, showing the movement between customer and supplier, then back, during the lifecycle. This shows the relationship between the design and build stages on the left arm of the 'V' and the test stages on the right arm of the 'V'.

The waterfall approach has both advantages and disadvantages.

Waterfall methods – advantages

- Documentation is well defined and hence auditable.
- Change control is simple to apply.

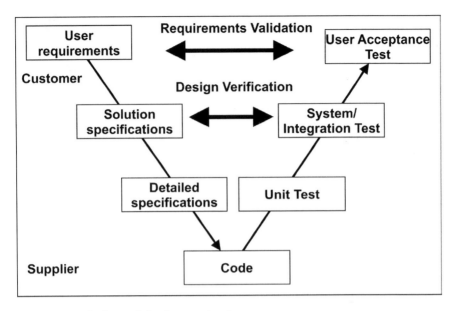

FIGURE 10.1 The 'V model' of system development

- Verification and validation are explicit steps in the process.
- Disruption of business as usual is minimised for the customer.
- The supplier's technical experts work in an efficient environment (their offices).
- Contract management is straightforward (but not necessarily easy).
- Complicated solutions can be broken down into components and spread across a large specialist workforce. If necessary, they can be developed by teams working anywhere in the world.

Waterfall methods – disadvantages

- Requirements capture is an intellectual exercise at the start of the project.
- The natural evolution of requirements in response to business changes may be missed.
- This approach is dependent on correct requirements documentation and change control.
- Definitive validation of the requirements only finishes at the end of the development. The limited engagement between the customer and the solution development team can mean requirement changes are missed until user acceptance test i.e. near the end of the project.

The biggest disadvantage of structured methods is that the solution is often found to not fit the **current** requirements during user acceptance testing. This is due

IT project quality management **147**

to original errors plus requirement changes that have not been captured. As this may be many months or even years after the start of the project, the scale of such discrepancies may be substantial, making them time-consuming and expensive to fix, or even causing the write-off of the project.

10.1.2 Incremental (Agile) methods

'Agile' methods are incremental, iterative methods that use successive time-limited ('Time-boxed') development periods ('Sprints') to move the solution functionality onwards. Given that structured methods have been around for many years, and clearly make logical sense, why have incremental methods become increasingly popular over the last 25 years?

One critical reason is the difficulty people find visualising the final IT solution, making it extremely difficult to capture true requirements. This means that at the start of the project, requirements are:

- Unlikely to be complete and accurate.
- Unlikely to exploit the potential that providing a new solution offers to transform the business process.
- Vulnerable to becoming outdated before the solution is delivered.
- Based on technology that is developing rapidly itself.

Incremental project development methods involve technical experts and business experts working together, side by side, in short steps known as 'sprints'. These are typically weeks rather than months in duration. During the sprints, both the overall requirements and the solution are developed. This means that development is phased, both in terms of the software and the vision of the solution. This is in contrast with the 'single step then corrections' of waterfall methods as shown in Figure 10.2.

When used effectively, incremental development reaches a satisfactory solution quicker and more reliably, but not necessarily more cheaply, than traditional methods.

In the early 1990s, an incremental approach known as rapid application development (RAD) was increasing in popularity, as the user interfaces for software applications evolved from text-only to today's graphical user interfaces (Apple, Windows). New software development tools enabled developers to demonstrate proposed solutions on-screen, rather than in documentation.

However, the RAD movement had reverted to the unstructured approach of the early days; there was no suitable quality management process to ensure quality products/deliverables.

The dynamic systems development method (DSDM) was created in 1995 as an end-to-end, user-centric but quality-controlled method for iterative and incremental development, striking a balance between large prescriptive methods and informal

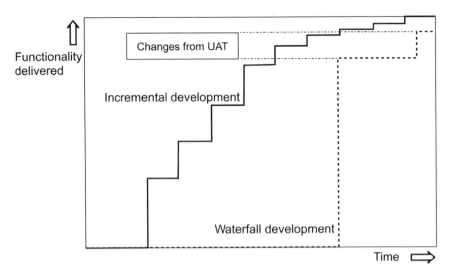

FIGURE 10.2 Progress comparison of Agile and Waterfall approaches

working (Richards, 2007). In 2007 a new 'free to view, free to use' version of the method, 'Atern', was released.

The eight principles of DSDM (DSDM Atern Handbook, 2008) are:

1. **Focus on the core business need**, with a sound business case, continuous business sponsorship and delivering against true business priorities.
2. **Always deliver on time**, by using time-boxing of the work and focusing on business priorities.
3. **Collaborate** with the right stakeholders at the right time, especially empowered business representatives, in a 'one team' culture.
4. **Never compromise on quality**: Design quality in, document it and test it appropriately.
5. **Build incrementally** from firm foundations, continually confirming the correct solution is being built and formally re-assessing priorities and project viability with each increment.
6. **Develop iteratively** with frequent delivery; build customer feedback into each iteration to converge on an effective business solution. Embrace change and be creative and experimental, most detail emerges later rather than sooner.
7. **Communicate continuously and clearly** across all project stakeholders, presenting iterations of the evolving solution early and often, keeping documentation lean and timely and managing stakeholder expectations throughout the project.
8. **Demonstrate control** with appropriate tracking and reporting and measuring progress through focus on delivery of tested products rather than completed activities.

RAD methods are now usually referred to as 'Agile' development. The explosion in popularity of Agile approaches (including DSDM, Scrum, Extreme Programming and several others) for IT development indicates that these approaches offer very real practical advantages over waterfall approaches in many situations. Agile approaches are now being applied to other types of project.

This approach has both advantages and disadvantages.

10.1.3 Incremental methods advantages

*   Requirements are developed continuously and cannot become out of date before solution delivery.
*   Validation of the requirements is continuous.
*   The potential of the new solution is explored incrementally.
*   The solution stays in step with technology that is rapidly developing.
*   Progress is relatively independent of correct documentation.
*   Constant engagement between the customer and the solution development team means requirement changes are rarely missed.

10.1.4 Incremental methods disadvantages

*   Despite DSDM, documentation may be poor (and un-auditable) – the code is the definitive documentation; any paperwork may have to be reverse-engineered.
*   Change control of paperwork is challenging to apply; change and configuration control of code is vital and must be effective and efficient.
*   Contract management can be challenging due to lack of reliable paperwork-verification and validation are not explicit steps.
*   Complicated solutions are not easily broken down into components that can be spread across a large specialist workforce or off-shored. The core development team must be broadly-skilled and work closely with the client. This may be co-located on-site or in a close-knit virtual environment.

10.1.5 Phased development

An alternative, three-phase approach to solutions design and development was developed by the authors at ICL in the late eighties, seeking the benefits of both incremental and Systems Engineering approaches.

The three phases are:

1. Proof of concept prototype – this is a requirements-gathering phase using incremental development of a working model, something that appears to work in the way expected, but without the underlying technical complexity. This can be done quickly and cheaply with high levels of customer engagement, validating the requirements.

150 IT project quality management

2. Technical demonstrator – this is done by the supplier to prove that the architecture chosen can support the functionality expressed in the working model.
3. Fully-engineered solution – given clear and correct requirements, and a proven architecture, the development of the final solution can go ahead quickly using a waterfall method but with low risk.

This approach has subsequently been used successfully in the defence solutions sector.

10.2 User interface design: including the user in the system

User interface design is particularly challenging when designing IT systems. This is primarily because of the wide range of operations that a user can perform. Microsoft Excel is an extreme example of flexibility, offering its user the ability to create very complicated and powerful applications without writing any code at all, but its user interface gives little or no indication to its users of what it is capable of, or how to achieve it.

Reflective exercise: what do people think of using computer systems – what's easy, what's hard, how does it vary between individuals?

User interfaces have two primary functions:

1. To present information to the user.
2. To collect input from the user.

From a quality perspective, the basic requirements are that the user interface design:

- Supports user effectiveness and efficiency in normal use of the system.
- Presents information in a format that is easily understood by a typical user.
- Minimises the chance of user error both in understanding the information displayed and entering information.
- Avoids user health implications such as repetitive strain injury and eye strain.
- Supports user response in the timescale needed if the system is real-time.
- Is easy to operate i.e. does not require intensive training that is quickly forgotten.
- In safety critical situations, filters the information presented to focus on that which is important.

This latter requirement may be overlooked in the system design and training, as described in Case study 31, where in a crisis, the user interface became unusable.

CASE STUDY 31: AIR FRANCE AIRBUS AF447 A330 LOST OVER SOUTH ATLANTIC, COMPILED FROM BEA (2012) AND MULTIPLE OTHER SOURCES

From its formation, Airbus used technical innovation to compete against established airliner manufacturers. It led in introducing 'fly by wire' control systems for civil airliners, replacing heavy and wear-prone physical connections between the pilots' controls and the aircraft's control surfaces with a computer-controlled electronic linkage. In normal circumstances, this has huge benefits both in safely piloting the aircraft and in its operational economics (minimising aircraft drag to reduce fuel consumption).

To get the best from flight control systems requires input from several sources besides the pilots' controls, the most important of which is airspeed, measured using a 'pitot head', and the A330 has three of these to achieve triple-redundancy.

Air France's A330 flight took off without the latest (high power anti-icing) pitot heads fitted. When the airliner flew into extreme icing conditions, the underpowered pitot head heaters failed to cope; all three heads are within inches of each other, subject to identical weather conditions, so all three pitot heads froze and the aircraft lost all airspeed data.

The catastrophe that followed shows how user interface design failed to deal with a safety critical situation

When the pitot heads froze, all functions within the flight control system that depended on airspeed started generating error messages and warnings, and then shut down. This initially bombarded the flight crew with detailed error messages then left them without any. The crew had not been trained to handle this scenario, and had to work out from first principles what the aircraft was doing, and why.

The junior, inexperienced pilot flying the aircraft made the wrong response to the situation, raising the nose (possibly unconsciously) and the aircraft climbed until eventually it stalled (the wings lost lift) at 38,000 ft. and the aircraft plunged down at nearly 10,000 ft. per minute until it hit the sea.

The other co-pilot was unable to identify the problem quickly and address it. What may have confused them was that after ignoring it at first, the stall warning horn stopped when the aircraft's nose pitched so far up that the stall warning system computer stopped 'believing' its inputs, but came back on every time the nose dropped as it returned into the 'belief zone', giving contrary feedback to the pilots.

152 IT project quality management

It is not certain why this scenario was not catered for in either the design or the training. Was the simultaneous failure of all three pitot heads inconceivable to the designers, even though their close physical proximity means a single impact such as a bird strike could disable all three? Like the Challenger O-ring failure, a single root cause resulted in multiple failures.

Improved User Interface was one of the recommendations in the final report by the French Civil Aviation Safety Investigation Authority (BEA, 2012).

Reflective exercise: are there examples in your work of poor user interface design?

10.3 Training to use IT solutions: people matter

Reflective exercise: what training do people get (a) in general (b) on IT? Compare and contrast — is IT training at the right level of thoroughness?

The third problem area for IT systems projects is user training. Construction activities such as welding, fabrication and excavator driving are clearly all skilled and require traditional training to develop the skill. Such training leads both to suitable skills being developed and to formal certification which is often mandatory for a role. Training is clearly linked to quality in this situation.

The introduction of a new computer system tends to impact significant numbers of current staff and there is rarely an opportunity to recruit staff with existing skills and experience. It demands a retraining programme for existing staff using the new system. Users are typically in one of two groups:

- Full-time users of the system, where it is the primary tool of the job for them.
- Part-time or occasional users of the system, such as supervisors and managers.

These two groups pose different challenges for delivering appropriate training.

10.3.1 Quality challenges in training full-time users

For people using the system hour after hour as part of their core role, their efficiency in using the system is important. As this is about core business processes, the challenges of training are simple, but involve all the regular users:

Change to business process – the new system will implement changes to the current business process. The users of the system must fully understand the new business process, why the changes are taking place, what the consequences are of user mistakes.

Scheduling training, availability of a training system – training may be mandated by a regulator or some other interested party; under those circumstances proving compliance requires that training be checked and tracked. Where large numbers of users are involved, training will need to be fitted into a tight time window (after a training environment becomes available and before go-live of the new system). This can create quite a challenge in maintaining 'business as usual' while large numbers of staff are being trained. It requires the cooperation of the staff affected by impacts of training on rotas and holidays. Effective engagement with any unions involved can be very beneficial.

Scope of training – there are likely to be multiple user groups that need training; this may require multiple variants of the training material, typically with common core material and tailored specialist content delivered through online tutorials or help material.

10.3.2 Quality challenges in training part-time users

Training in IT of managers is often a low priority; they are often expected to pick up the use of IT systems with little or no training. The best example of this expectation is the use of office suites such as Microsoft Office. These fantastically complex and versatile tools are used by people who frequently understand less than 10 per cent of what that tool can do, having 'just picked up the basics'. The substantial challenges in educating part-time users include:

- Getting training considered at all.
- Agreeing the scope of training – covering users' diverse set of needs.
- Making reference material available – information targeted at different needs.
- Overcoming the forgetting curve – it is easy to forget how to do something complex that is only done occasionally.

Training part-time and casual users of new systems is challenging because of the diversity of their requirements. Training takes time and effort to schedule and deliver – casual users are likely to miss courses or find they don't focus on their needs. Managers may have other demands on their time taking priority over IT training.

This can be addressed by providing a programme of 'drop in' training sessions for those who want them, backed up by on-line tutorials and user guides.

10.4 Performance and other non-functional requirements often missed

The fourth problem area for IT projects is non-functional requirements, especially interactive performance – the speed with which the system responds to user input like a key press or mouse click. Although computer processors are thousands of times more powerful today than in the first PC in the 1980s, computers don't really appear to work any faster. In some cases, operations seem slower and more 'clunky'. Part of the reason is that computers are doing much more work running the complicated user interface and operating system. The other part of the answer is that developers worry less about making things work as quickly as possible. This perhaps results from the realisation that people are relatively happy to wait for responses over the Internet and response time is not the key issue. In most networked solutions, the delay while the data is being transferred over the network for each interaction is typically thousands of times longer than the time the computer would take to access it on its own hard drive.

This does not mean responsiveness has become unimportant, quite the opposite. Most of people's interactions with computer systems are transactional with little or no thinking time; any noticeable delay in the way the computer responds is an interference with smooth use, and reduces efficiency. Pausing, freezing etc. often result in frustration, buttons being clicked repeatedly, leading to 'user errors'. Real-time responsiveness becomes even more important when managing/controlling safety-critical systems e.g. combat systems, plant control systems and vehicle control systems. Speed of response is an important requirement to specify correctly. Personal experience suggests that contact centres are rarely equipped with IT that is fast enough!

The requirements for speed of response must be evaluated carefully, and the product proven to meet them through specific performance testing.

Other important non-functional requirements to be considered include:

- Availability – how often, and for how long, will the system be down for scheduled maintenance and off-line processing?
- Reliability – what is the maximum acceptable frequency and duration of outage due to unscheduled maintenance/bugs?
- Maintainability – what skills and effort are required to maintain the system running smoothly, how long will the storage take to fill up and how easy is it to extend?
- Security – what access control of users to data, traceability of changes are needed?
- How many concurrent users and registered users must the system support?

These requirements vary enormously between a Word Processor, a credit card processing system and an airliner flight control system. The context of the system usage makes it essential to document these requirements.

As with performance, these requirements must be evaluated carefully and the product proven to meet them through specific operational acceptance testing (OAT).

10.5 Safety-critical and control systems requirements

Safety-critical systems and control systems also have a set of requirements that are particularly important for IT systems. These are detailed in Table 9.1.

Behavioural safety is about people working in a way that is as safe as they can make it (Geller, 2004). Examples of this are holding onto the handrail on stairs, reversing into parking bays and always wearing the correct safety equipment.

Functional safety (IEC 61508) requires that the designs of equipment and processes optimise safety. This is particularly important for real-time monitoring and control systems. Functional safety is system-wide, and has to extend to the parts of the system that are controlled and monitored, not just the control systems themselves.

Functional safety assessment typically includes:

1. Identifying the required safety functions.
2. Assessing the risk-reduction required end-to-end.
3. Verifying safety function performance, especially under failure and error conditions.
4. Conducting audits to confirm the right functional safety management standards are being used.

Both behavioural and functional safety need to be assessed holistically in the context of the system as a whole, not just at specific points, within the environment in which the system operates.

10.6 Testing and accepting IT solutions

The final topic that is particularly problematic for IT projects is testing and acceptance. With the exception of the user interface design, which has a substantial subjective component in its assessment, the quality methods applied to Information Technology solutions are primarily based on extensive testing rather than inspection.

This creates quite a challenge; meeting the requirements must be assessed by a comprehensive set of tests, each including a set of test scenarios and test cases, with input data and expected output data. As the complexity of the system increases, the number of test cases required to adequately test the solution rises disproportionately – this is known as the '**combinatorial explosion**'. This makes exhaustive testing of complicated systems impractical at best and impossible at worst.

TABLE 10.1 Safety-critical and control systems special requirements

Area	Requirement	Impact if not met	Illustration
Speed of response	Usually (near) real-time response.	Inputs get out of sync, output and oscillations are amplified instead of damped.	Snaking wagon or caravan going out of control on a motorway.
Safety criticality	Fail-safe design – failure of a control system element must leave the situation safe.	Failure of the control system can lead to the plant or equipment becoming uncontrollable (or at least uncontrolled).	Train braking systems keep the brakes **off**. Any failure in the braking systems causes the train to stop.
	Decision-support in dangerous situations from clear unambiguous information.	Control is the difference between a nuclear power plant and Chernobyl. Control by malcontents is a loss of control by the legitimate users.	3 Mile Island – valve positions were not displayed from direct monitoring sensors. Inferred positions were incorrect, leading to mismanagement and the worst nuclear incident in US history.
	Security – access by malcontents prevented.		9/11, World Trade Centre – inadequate physical security for airliner controls.
Reliability	Minimise unplanned shut-downs, with gentle degradation of performance when faults occur.	Emergency shut-down.	Loss of HMS Coventry – under air attack a missile system fell over at the point of firing and had to be rebooted. Bombs sank HMS Coventry.
Longevity	The control system must be capable of being maintained over its working life, often decades, allowing replacement of obsolete components by current technology.	Major replacement expense. In the case of control systems in aircraft, ships, cars etc., it is simply uneconomical to replace them.	Failure of Concorde's air intake ramp controller would force it to divert immediately. They were too expensive to replace, attrition lead to fewer controller sets than actual aircraft. Controllers must be transferred between aircraft to keep them airworthy.

Availability	Minimise planned shutdowns.	Planned shut-down.	Power station – Loss of production costs well over £1m per week per unit.
Certification by regulators	The system must be testable and proven to meet the standard of the regulator.	Not licensed to operate the product.	The RAF's "special forces" Chinook HC3 helicopters were fitted with a mission management system that was not testable so no certificate of airworthiness could be issued.
Data collection	Collect, log and analyse operational parameters in great detail, allowing quality improvements in operation and maintenance.	Lost opportunity for quality improvement and post-event analysis.	SCADA (System Control and Data Acquisition) packages are commercially available as standard solutions.
Operator errors	Minimise operator errors.	Unnecessary mistakes.	Most of the case studies on this book!

158 IT project quality management

The extreme test cases from a business perspective may differ substantially from the extreme cases technically. Testing for the business priorities and coverage may not be exercising the extremes of the system capability, so may miss defects that appear in unusual business scenarios.

The use of techniques like state-based programming and object-orientation help enormously to build in constraints on software behaviour, making it more robust and predictable. These techniques are now part of the Universal Modeling Language (UML) maintained by the Object Management Group and standardised as an ISO standard (ISO, 2005).

The common systematic test model consists of the types of testing in Table 10.2:

The application of tests in the waterfall model is straightforward, as described in the V-model (with operational acceptance commonly running concurrently with user acceptance).

The application of testing in Agile approaches is less straightforward. If each development iteration is sufficiently substantial, all types of testing should be applied to it. Small iterations may take a risk-based approach and reduce the scope of testing.

10.6.1 Random testing explores 'beyond the envelope'

Testing should always include carefully structured test plans with well-defined and detailed test scripts to verify that the requirements have been met. However, they do not guarantee fitness for purpose and can miss defects, especially those that cause problems when user errors happen.

'Random' testing (also known as 'monkey' testing) can quickly identify where the solution design doesn't include adequate trapping and handling of unexpected

TABLE 10.2 Breakdown of IT test types

Test type	Scope	Coverage
Unit	Individual module	Exhaustive functional test of module
System	Modules linked	Exhaustive functional test of system where feasible
Integration	Systems working together	Exhaustive functional testing of interfaces, sample testing of end-to-end transactions/processes
Operational acceptance	Complete solution	Non-functional testing; includes performance, security etc.
Regression	Any level, after changes to the solution	Standard test suite covering existing functionality – confirms that existing functionality has not been broken by changes
User Acceptance	Business testing of the complete solution	Sample testing of the full scope and intensive testing focused by business priority

IT project quality management **159**

CASE STUDY 32: MANAGEMENT INFORMATION SYSTEM

A new system had been developed for a government agency to give the Director direct access to all project financial data. The system had successfully completed its planned functional acceptance tests, but was encountering an operational problem with database locking. Extensive diagnostic testing had resulted in a 'fix' being applied, and the new system version was being retested.

As the problem was after the system's implementation, the original test manager had moved on and a new test manager was assigned. In addition to the two days of planned tests, which had all been passed successfully, he ran a brief session of random testing with one of the client's testers. Within 10 minutes, they had recreated the problem, and within a further 20 minutes had identified the exact scenario under which it occurred. This led to a permanent fix of the problem.

---

scenarios, particularly those coming from users doing things outside the documented requirements.

Random testing is an approach which requires the tester to key in actions that **don't** align with the requirements, simulating user errors. Such testing can quickly reveal faults and missing safeguards in the system design. As an example of this, clerks accidentally hitting 'Shift\' instead of just 'Shift', when keying in customer addresses, completely disrupted one company's data warehouse which was very difficult to solve. This type of keying error is very unlikely to be included in a test script, as its effect was completely unrelated to data entry functionality.

A random testing success is described in Case study 32.

10.7 Conclusions of chapter

This chapter concludes that different methodologies are appropriate for different types of IT project, and a hybrid approach may be appropriate.

It shows that good design of the user interface is vital to successful solutions, especially in high-performance environments like contact centres, and in safety-critical situations.

Appropriate training is essential to get the most from an IT solution.

Non-functional requirements being overlooked creates a serious risk to the project, as under-performance in these areas can be more damaging to benefit delivery than limitations in functionality.

Safety-critical and control systems have special requirements that must be addressed by the design of the solution.

The test programme needs careful design to ensure that requirements are validated as early as possible, and verification of requirements being met allows stage payments to be made.

160 IT project quality management

IT solutions are particularly susceptible to early constraints on time and budget, as they are usually complex, and if their requirements are not well-understood, the solution delivered will require expensive and time-consuming rectification, perhaps even cancellation of the project.

10.8 Bibliography

BEA (2012) – https://www.bea.aero/docspa/2009/f-cp090601.en/pdf/f-cp090601.en.pdf

BSI, (2015) 'BS EN ISO 9000:2015 Quality management systems, Fundamentals and Vocabulary', British Standards Institution, ISBN: 9780580788789

DSDM Atern Handbook (2008) – https://www.agilebusiness.org/content/atern-principles

Geller, E. Scott (2004). 'Behavior-based safety: a solution to injury prevention: behavior-based safety "empowers" employees and addresses the dynamics of injury prevention', Risk & Insurance 15 (12, 01 Oct) p. 66

IEC 61508 (2010) 'Functional Safety of Electrical/Electronic/Programmable Electronic Safety-related Systems (E/E/PE, or E/E/PES)', Parts 1–7, IEC

ISO (2005) 'Universal Modeling Language (UML)' ISO/IEC 19501:2005 (OMG-UML VER 1.3)

Richards, K. (2007) 'Agile project management: running PRINCE2 projects with DSDM Atern' Office of Government Communication, TSO, ISBN: 9780113310586

Further reading

Augustine, S. (2005) 'Managing Agile Projects', Prentice Hall PTR, London, ISBN: 0-131-24071-4

Weaver, P., Lambrou, N. and Walkley, M. (2002) 'Practical Business Systems Development using SSADM: A Complete Tutorial Guide', FT Prentice Hall, London, ISBN: 0-273-65575-2

11

THE ROLE OF PUBLISHED STANDARDS IN ACHIEVING PROJECT QUALITY

Standards are often seen as the core of quality management. Published international quality standards represent the distilled wisdom and experience of a world-wide team of experts, and allow supply chains to span the globe with confidence.

We have left them until last because published quality management standards also carry a risk – they can become strait-jackets if compliance with them becomes the end in itself, hindering business agility and growth. An established feature of many industries is customers requiring that suppliers are certified as compliant to quality standards like ISO 9001, which may have resulted in 'quality' often being seen as a bureaucracy; a 'necessary evil' rather than adding huge value.

Standards can't impose quality in an environment that doesn't welcome them. Published standards exist to guide and support organisations, but can easily become dogma instead. Blind adherence to quality standards can prevent the appropriate balance being struck between time, cost and quality. Unnecessary compliance to quality standards creates a significant bureaucratic overhead. In one instance, applying inappropriate standards resulted in a simple trolley for carrying a piece of scientific equipment being assessed to the same standard as the equipment itself (and failing).

Like all tools, quality standards are powerful when used appropriately and dangerous when misused. Following a quality standard when it is inappropriate can damage a project, and ignoring it when it is essential can cause project failure.

This chapter briefly introduces the key ISO standards relevant to setting up a quality management system in an organisation and applying quality management in projects. It also touches briefly on product quality standards. It explores performance baselining to help improve project management performance. Standard Operating Procedures are useful and versatile aids to improving both efficiency and effectiveness – their development and use is discussed.

162 The role of published standards in achieving project quality

Learning outcomes for the chapter

On completing this chapter, the reader will understand that:

- International Standards exist to support effectiveness in delivering quality.
- Standard operating procedures are a powerful tool to deliver both effectiveness and efficiency through supporting quality processes.
- Maturity models allow weaknesses to be identified and fixed.
- Standards alone can't ensure quality.

11.1 Standards supporting quality management

A suite of International Standards Organisation (ISO) Standards has been published to address quality management. The UK participated in the preparation of these standards and the British Standards Institution (BSI) republishes the official English language versions of the ISO standards.

International standards that relate to project quality management are principally:

1. BS EN ISO 9000 Quality management systems – Fundamentals and vocabulary.
2. BS EN ISO 9001 Quality management systems – Requirements.
3. BS EN ISO 9004 Managing for the sustained success of an organisation — a quality management approach.
4. BS EN ISO 19011 Guidelines for quality and/or environmental management systems auditing.
5. BS ISO 10006 Quality management systems — Guidelines for quality management in projects.

Quality standards relating to products, rather than to quality processes, are addressed later in this chapter.

11.1.1 ISO 9000 – Quality management systems – Fundamentals and vocabulary

BS EN ISO 9000:2015, updated in 2015, 'describes the fundamental concepts and principles of quality management' and goes on to list of potential beneficiaries it is applicable to:

It introduces and defines these concepts:

1. Quality.
2. Quality Management System (QMS).
3. Context of an organisation.
4. Interested parties.
5. Support.

The role of published standards in achieving project quality **163**

It then lays down the quality management principles for management to lead the organisation towards improved performance:

a) Customer focus.
b) Leadership.
c) Engagement of people.
d) Process approach.
e) Improvement.
f) Evidence-based decision making.
g) Relationship management.

It then describes how to develop a QMS using fundamental concepts and principles, and how that relates to QMS standards, other management systems and excellence models, before moving on to the core content, 'Terms and definitions'.

11.1.2 ISO 9001 – Quality management systems – Requirements

BS EN ISO 9001:2015, 'promotes the adoption of a process approach when developing, implementing and improving the effectiveness of a quality management system, to enhance customer satisfaction by meeting customer requirements.' It is based on the principles and concepts described in ISO 9000.

The 2015 revision has been restructured in line with other ISO management systems standards, and substantially strengthens the emphasis on risk-based thinking, while increasing flexibility.

It is focused at the organisation level, not the project level, and states that the adoption of a quality management system should be a strategic decision of an organisation. It proposes the benefits to an organisation implementing a QMS based on the standard are:

a. The ability to consistently provide products and services that meet customer and applicable statutory and regulatory requirements.
b. Facilitating opportunities to enhance customer satisfaction.
c. Addressing risks and opportunities associated with its context and objectives.
d. The ability to demonstrate conformity to specified quality management system requirements.

It re-affirms a process approach to quality management based on the Deming Cycle of continuous improvement and risk-based thinking then goes on to address:

1. The context of the organisation.
2. Leadership (and responsibilities at all levels).
3. Planning for quality (including risks/opportunities).
4. Support requirements, competences and processes.
5. Operations and the embedding of quality into them.

164 The role of published standards in achieving project quality

6. Performance evaluation of the resulting quality.
7. Improvement, building performance incrementally.

11.1.3 ISO 9004 – Managing for the sustained success of an organisation — A quality management approach

BS EN ISO 9004:2009 'provides guidelines that consider both the effectiveness and efficiency of the quality management system. The aim of this standard is improvement of the performance of the organisation and satisfaction of customers and other interested parties.'

It aims to give guidance on achieving sustained success through:

- The effective management of the organisation.
- Awareness of the organisation's environment.
- Learning from experience.
- Appropriate application of improvements and/or innovations.
- Self-assessment of the quality maturity level of the organisation, feeding into continuous improvement.

It covers a broader scope than ISO 9001:

- Extending resource management.
- Including strategy and policy.
- Including improvement, innovation and learning.
- Extending monitoring, measurement, analysis and review.
- Including process management.

11.1.4 ISO 19011 – Guidelines for quality and/or environmental management systems auditing

BS EN ISO 19011:2002 'provides guidance on auditing quality and environmental management systems.'

Auditing, especially of tier 1 suppliers and, where appropriate, their supply chain, is a vital tool in project quality management. BS EN ISO 19011 helps auditing by:

- Combining quality and environmental audits in a single programme.
- Minimising disruption to normal activities.
- Streamlining the audit process.
- Reducing paperwork.
- Following best practice during audits.

The standard provides:

- A clear explanation of the principles of management systems auditing.

The role of published standards in achieving project quality **165**

- Guidance on the management of audit programmes.
- Guidance on the conduct of internal or external audits.
- Advice on the competence and evaluation of auditors.

11.1.5 ISO 10006 – Quality management systems — Guidelines for quality management in projects

BS EN 10006:2003 takes the principles and terminology from ISO 9000 and 9001 and fine-tunes them for application to the project environment. It defines and details:

1. Project characteristics.
2. Organisations.
3. Processes within projects.
4. Phases in projects.
5. Project quality management systems, especially quality planning.
6. Management responsibility, including commitment, strategic process according to the eight principles laid down in ISO 9000, management reviews and progress evaluations.
7. Resource management.
8. Product realisation.

11.1.6 Product quality standards

Product quality standards were originally introduced to give buyers confidence in the quality of the products being purchased without tedious and expensive quality assurance activities. There are a range of quality marks in use around the world. These include, in the USA, the FCC compliance mark for electromagnetic interference, NTA Inc. for building materials, and Energy Star for energy efficient electronic goods. In Japan, there is the Japanese Industrial Standards mark, in India the ISI mark, the JAC-ANZ mark in Australia and New Zealand and the CSA Mark in Canada.

In the UK – Kitemark

A product with a Kitemark (Figure 11.1) has been independently tested by BSI, the British Standards Institute. This is a registered certification mark owned and operated by BSI, which confirms that the product conforms to the relevant British Standard, and the company has been issued a BSI license to use the Kitemark for that product. Retesting is annually at least.

Display of the Kitemark is not mandatory.

Purchasing or specifying Kitemarked products or services for projects provides extra quality assurance. Example Kitemark classifications include construction, electrical, fire and personal protective equipment.

166 The role of published standards in achieving project quality

FIGURE 11.1 The BS kitemark

In the European Economic Area – the CE mark

The CE mark (Figure 11.2) is a declaration by a manufacturer that their product meets all the appropriate provisions in the relevant European Directives.

FIGURE 11.2 The CE mark

In specific circumstances, CE marking may be mandatory. Independent assessment may be mandatory; if not, the manufacturer's unverified claim is acceptable and a supplier can be prosecuted for a false claim.

Independent assessment must be done by a 'notified body', e.g. BSI, which is an organisation that has been nominated by a member government and notified by the European Commission.

11.2 Project management maturity and performance improvement

Project performance improvement needs a clear understanding of where project management is performing well, and where it is under-performing. There are three main performance measures of project management:

1. The effectiveness of the project – does it achieve the desired results?
2. The efficiency of the project – does it deliver economically?
3. The maturity of the project's management – does it operate reliably and reproducibly?

The key indicators of project management maturity (Nicholson, 2006) are generic but relate clearly to quality management. Nicholson suggests 8 areas are indicators of maturity. Each of the areas has a target value and a measure. Organisations are recommended to assess their performance in each of these areas when benchmarking their project management performance. The areas identified as indicators of project management maturity are:

- Risk management:
    a. Target: No issue occurs where the risk hasn't been fully managed; that is to say, issues only arise when identified risks occur and the project has mitigation and contingency plans in place.
    b. Measure: Number of issues arising not identified and mitigated as risks.
- Project cost performance:
    a. Target: Costs remain within identified tolerance without compromising time or quality of project delivery, requiring that the budget includes contingency for quality issues.
    b. Measure: cost variance outside tolerance in financial terms for the whole project.
- Project schedule performance:
    - Target: Progress of project delivery remains within tolerance without compromising cost or quality, requiring that the schedule includes contingency for quality issues.
    - Measure: time variance of the project's milestones outside tolerance.
- Return on investment (ROI):
    - Target: ROI remains within the tolerances set in the business case.
    - Measure: ROI variance outside tolerance.

        Benefits realisation is a key element of planning (now considered to be at the programme level) often over-looked; an otherwise successful project failing to deliver planned benefits (through its parent programme) also fails.

- Staffing:
    - Target: Good morale within the project team.
    - Measure: response to an Employee Satisfaction Survey.
- Learning from Project Post Mortems:
    - Target: mistakes made in previous projects are not repeated.
    - Measure: Cost of errors already listed in Lessons Learned reports.
- Effective Governance and Strategic Alignment:
    - Target: the right project is done at the right time.
    - Measure: Cost of inappropriate projects.
- Customer Satisfaction:
    - Target: the project delivers the benefits the customer expects, within tolerance.
    - Measure: Rework costs to the project and delays where the customer expectations are not aligned with project delivery.

168 The role of published standards in achieving project quality

Project management maturity is covered in more detail by Terry Cooke-Davis (2004).

11.3 Benefiting from Standard Operating Procedures (SOPs)

A standard operating procedure (SOP) is a set of documented instructions that define a routine, repetitive activity. SOPs provide the right information to perform the job properly and consistently, supporting conformance to requirements, and collecting any quality data needed. Alternative terms such as 'protocols' and 'worksheets' may be used instead of SOPs (EPA, 2007).

11.3.1 Benefits of using SOPs

SOPs support good quality through consistently correct application of processes and tools to minimise variation, independent of the individuals involved. Their additional benefits include:

- Having SOPs is part of many regulatory requirements and standards.
- Contributing to induction and training.
- Improving communication and reducing safety risks.
- Reducing errors and rework.
- Providing a quality audit trail.

Projects will normally apply or revise pre-existing SOPs, but the production of new SOPs may be necessary, e.g. where new equipment or systems are being introduced.

11.3.2 Challenges in using SOPs effectively

To deliver any value, SOPs must be **followed/used**; sitting on the shelf gathering dust, they are worthless. The need to follow SOPs must be ingrained in the culture of the organisation. This means their use must be monitored frequently and any failure to use investigated, and corner-cutting visibly addressed.

To make them easy to use, SOPs should be:

- As brief as possible, without losing key detail.
- Step-wise, with enough detail to follow easily, with a flowchart if necessary.
- Written in simple, plain language with clear diagrams where needed.
- In the correct medium for the point of use (paper, plastic-covered, electronic etc).
- Easily accessible where the work is to be done.
- Always kept up-to-date.

If this is not the case, employees will have a legitimate excuse not to use the standard procedures. The following challenges in exploiting SOPs are adapted from the US Environmental Protection Agency (EPA) (2007):

The role of published standards in achieving project quality **169**

- Creating a SOP may involve reconciling conflicting views and creating a new process to replace existing working practices.
- Access to the SOP may be difficult in some working environments.
- Instilling the need to follow the relevant SOPs takes time and effort.
- Ensuring the SOP is always used requires active supervision until it becomes habit.
- Making sure paper checklists and other forms used when the SOP is applied are always available at the time and place they are needed.

> *Reflective exercise: when should SOPs be used? What are your organisation's SOPs called? Are your organisation's SOPs good? Could they be improved? How?*

11.4 Conclusion: standards support delivering quality, but can't ensure it

Good quality management underpins project success.

This chapter considers how applying appropriate published quality standards correctly will save time and money overall through creating a quality management system that delivers quality products and outcomes consistently.

It explores the risk that the up-front investments of time and effort in quality can be seen as unnecessary, leading to corner-cutting. It warns that inappropriate application of standards can create cost and delay penalties, as 'gold-plating' of requirements leads to products that at best are too expensive and slow to procure, and at worst, completely unfit for purpose when delivered.

The ISO standards relevant to setting up a quality management system in an organisation and applying quality management in projects are a valuable resource to guide organisations in setting up internal processes and standards to support quality working.

Maturity models and performance baselining can help improve project management performance, but are dependent on an organisational culture willing to invest in them.

Standard Operating Procedures are quick, cheap, useful and versatile aids to improving both efficiency and effectiveness. Engaging their users in creating and maintaining them is often a way to ensure their use.

No processes or standards can deliver quality if people don't apply them effectively. Creating and supporting a quality culture is the accountability of executive management, but is the responsibility of management at all levels.

11.5 Bibliography

Bartlett, J. (2005) 'Right First and Every Time: Managing Quality in Projects and Programmes', Project Manager Today Publications, Bramshill, Hants, ISBN: 1-900391-13-9

170 The role of published standards in achieving project quality

Cooke-Davies, T. (2004) 'Project Management Maturity Models', in 'The Wiley Guide to Managing Projects', Eds P. W. G. Morris and J. K. Pinto, John Wiley & Sons, Inc. Print ISBN: 9780471233022 Online ISBN: 9780470172391

EPA (2007) 'Guidance for Preparing Standard Operating Procedures (SOPs)' EPA QA/G-6 U.S. Environmental Protection Agency – https://www.epa.gov/sites/production/files/2015-06/documents/g6-final.pdf

Nicholson, L. (2006) 'Project Management Benchmarking for Measuring Capability within the Organisation', PM World Today – December 2006 (Vol. VIII, Issue 12) 'Connecting the World of Project Management'

12

PROJECT SUCCESS AND BALANCING THE IRON TRIANGLE

The 'Iron Triangle' was proposed by Martin Barnes as a tool to facilitate creating a shared understanding of the relative priorities of time, cost and quality in achieving a successful outcome.

This chapter considers the original use of the iron triangle as an analytical tool to create a shared understanding of the project balance, and concludes on the value of quality focus on project success.

Learning outcomes for the chapter

On completing this chapter, the reader will understand that:

- The iron triangle is an analytical tool for balancing priorities.
- Some project circumstances are used as excuses to ignore quality disciplines.
- Quality management is essential for successful projects, more than repaying its investment.

12.1 The iron triangle as a tool, balancing quality against time and cost

The triangle is a map of the time, cost and quality priority space, in which the project can be positioned.

Getting the project sponsor and the project team together to agree the most appropriate target point on the map for the project creates an explicit understanding of what trade-offs regarding quality are acceptable for project success, and how quality failures are likely to increase costs and delays.

Since its inception in the late 1960s, the triangle model has been adopted by professional bodies and key textbooks as a way of expressing the various criteria that

172 Project success and balancing the iron triangle

a project has to satisfy. There is a general agreement that two of the criteria that the project has to satisfy are 'time' and 'cost' being the deadline for project completion and the project budget. However, the third element of the triangle has a disputed lineage being variously termed as 'quality', 'scope' and 'performance'.

In a widely-cited paper, Atkinson (1999) disputes that the triangle model is adequate and suggests that for a project to be viewed as a success, it is not the quality of the artefact resulting from the project but the customer satisfaction and the benefits accrued from using the artefact that are the real measures of project success. This approach is followed by other authors who also studied the concept of project success and how it is measured both from a 'client' and a 'contractor' perspective.

In our view, this focus on using the triangle for measurement misses the original intention for its use. In a paper presented at the University of Manchester in 2013, Dr Barnes made clear that the triangle was intended to be used as a means of achieving a shared viewpoint, reconciling the interests of various stakeholders in a project team. He explained that, in using the triangle model, he would bring key stakeholders into a room, display the image of the 'Time, Cost and Quality' triangle on screen and ask stakeholders to agree where the project focus should be. Is it on achieving the deadline with cost and quality as secondary constraints? Is it on finishing on budget with the deadline and quality as secondary constraints? Is it on the project quality? Depending on the answer, the question will give a different approach to decisions on the project. In today's leadership terms, this is the project's 'true North', a point that all can agree is the direction of travel.

Taking this view of the triangle as more of a project compass than a yardstick for measuring progress, gives a way of viewing different project scenarios or situations.

Figure 12.1 shows how we have split the iron triangle into seven approximate zones, which are analysed in Table 12.1. The different zones are characteristic of

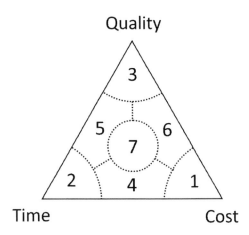

FIGURE 12.1 The iron triangle, split into zones for quality management impact assessment

TABLE 12.1 Quality management assessment of zones in the Barnes Triangle

Zone	Nature	Typical projects	Quality Impact	Quality Approach
1	Cost is everything – time and quality must give	Very rare in reality; reflects poor governance, as business benefits come from time and quality. Buying a house typically comes closest – the best we can afford	Cost focus will damage quality work, leading to delays and cost overruns, hence failure	Get the project on a more balanced basis – if this is not possible, get it cancelled
2	Immovable deadline – do what is necessary to hit it	Regulatory compliance needed to stay in business External constraints force urgent change	Rushing may well result in poor design and corner cutting, reducing quality	Make it clear that good quality planning makes it MORE LIKELY the target will be hit
3	Requirements must be met, however slowly or expensively	Nuclear (historically) Status (Scottish Parliament, aircraft carriers) Do change control well!	Seems ideal, but people will still complain about costs and slippages	Take the opportunity to do good quality planning, then deliver as quickly and cheaply as possible
4	Time and cost immovable, quality must give	Strategic projects being authorised by customers not in touch with reality – poor governance, as the business benefits come from quality	Cost/time focus will damage quality work, leading to delays and cost overruns, hence failure	Make it clear that good quality planning makes project success **more** likely
5	Deadline is fixed, quality must be met, sponsor is prepared to pay	Curing the "Millennium Bug" was one example The 2012 London Olympics was another.	Perceived Pressure to rush into things, but the quality requirement means that planning is vital	Make it clear that good quality planning makes project success more likely
6	Quality must be delivered within budget, but no hurry	Usually a proactive strategic change from good governance, where the benefits largely result from quality. The billing migration case study was one of these	Ideal zone – no time pressure to interfere with quality planning	Plan quality thoroughly, then use to deliver on budget and earlier than expected
7	An evenly-balanced situation – everything is negotiable to deliver success	Major projects that don't involve downtime for the business e.g. IT upgrades	Pressure to rush into things and cut costs, but the quality requirement means that quality carries real weight	Make it clear that good quality planning makes it MORE LIKELY the target will be hit

174 Project success and balancing the iron triangle

different types of project, and we argue that each leads to a different attitude to project quality management.

The different zones have very different impacts on quality management priorities.

Analysing extensive first-hand project experience, plus a wide range of projects in the public domain, it is clear that some types of project are at a particularly high risk of poor quality delivery. If we look at where the pressure against quality investment is greatest, it seems intuitively obvious that it is in the zones opposite the 'quality corner' of the triangle:

- Zone 1: cost is everything – time and quality must give.
- Zone 2: immovable deadline – do what is necessary to hit it.
- Zone 4: time and cost immovable, quality must give.

However, these are not equally threatening to quality management.

- Zone 1: Cost is everything – time and quality must give

In **Zone 1**, where cost is the primary driver, and no tight time constraints prevent quality planning, the limitation on quality working is spending on resource. Intelligent project management, focusing on quality at the start of the project, can create a quality management approach that doesn't require noticeable additional resource, as it is woven into the way of working. The cost of implementing quality can be minimised by paying attention to this at the early stages of the project - with good quality planning, and negotiating supplier quality into the contracts.

'Time' can therefore be traded for quality; allowing the schedule to be extended to deliver a quality outcome within minimum budget. In a programme led by an author, there was plenty of time before the deadline, and this was used to optimise the approach progressively, driving down the cost of the project by 30 per cent against its original estimate, and reducing defect rates virtually to zero.

Reconsidering the business objectives and requirements can sometimes reveal a completely different solution that can be delivered more quickly and cheaply than the one originally proposed. In one project, a change of approach from a technical solution to a change of working practices meant that a complex piece of technology was not needed.

Approaches to escalating costs in projects in Zone 1 are sometimes solved by 'de-scoping' the project. This may be the reason that 'scope' is sometimes envisaged as the third element of the triangle. However, any de-scoping or value engineering exercise must ensure that the project requirements are still met.

- Zone 2: immovable deadline – do what is necessary to hit it.

In **Zone 2**, although the project deadline is immovable, the project doesn't suffer from budget limits preventing quality working. All the necessary resource can be

Project success and balancing the iron triangle **175**

brought on board, empowering early quality planning. The threat to quality here is that time pressure means that early progress needs to be made visible for many stakeholders. Failure to do this can lead to rushing into delivery with insufficient focus on planning. Paradoxically, this can cause delays when the early work is based on incorrect assumptions. The typical saying related to this, 'More haste, less speed', indicates the problem has been around for a long time.

An approach we have found effective on several projects is based on critical path analysis. Critical path long-lead-time items are addressed as the priority, using appropriate resource. This demonstrates to stakeholders that the project is under control and that progress is being made, with a focus on completing on time. Concurrently, the remaining resource in the project team carries out thorough quality planning for the other elements.

This approach aims to minimise overall risk to project success by minimising quality risks on non-urgent work, while avoiding slippage to the critical path.

Active risk management of those critical path items is essential. Since financial constraints are low, budget can be expended on managing these risks, both in mitigation and contingency options.

*   Zone 4: time and cost immovable, quality must give.

Zone 4, with no flexibility of the deadline or the budget is the true nightmare scenario. With no slack anywhere but in quality, this can only be addressed by reducing the scope while still delivering a quality solution. Value engineering to reduce cost is rarely an option when time-pressure is high. Unfortunately, the cost savings from reducing scope often result in disproportionate benefit reductions too, which can destroy the business case. If reducing a bridge from six lanes to four lanes reduces its cost by 20 per cent, it reduces its capacity by considerably more. There is also the question of whether scope reduction would result in an effective solution – 100 per cent of a bridge or nuclear power station is needed to deliver ANY benefit at all – partial completion has no value.

In two successive cases in this zone, the project sponsors had each personally committed to delivering business benefits in a tight timescale, within a fixed budget, BEFORE the feasibility study and supplier selection. Their personal credibility was at stake, so neither timescale nor the budget was negotiable. When it became clear that these commitments could not be met, the sponsors' reactions were similar – denial, anger and a series of reactions that led to complete collapse of their programme.

Having seen programmes and projects in this zone fail persistently, it is vital to move the project from this zone into either of zones 1 or 2 through stakeholder engagement. Depending on their relative priorities, either more time must be allowed to deliver within budget by developing a more cost-effective solution, or more budget must be allocated to fund a more expensive but effective project.

176 Project success and balancing the iron triangle

Zone 7: everything is negotiable

Zone 7, where time, cost and quality are evenly balanced, can still be a problem for quality management, as progress in time and budget are much more **visible** to stakeholders due to the simplicity of their measurement and presentation. Earned Value techniques try to address this, and are a powerful tool to use if the right progress measures are applied. However, these measures carry their own cost, and rely on building in suitable quality assurance/control measures so that progress is not over-estimated.

All the zones have different priorities, but in **none** of them is quality unimportant — quality is about delivering a solution that is fit for purpose, and all projects have to do that, whatever their other priorities:

- A project that has a tight budget cannot afford to waste money on delays or rework.
- A project with a critical deadline cannot afford delays from rework, retesting and mistakes.
- A project with demanding quality standards cannot afford to over-specify components to the point that they don't work together as a system.

12.2 Conclusion: a culture of quality is needed to balance the iron triangle for project success

We have explored how delivering quality products is essential for project success. We have considered how the partitioning of responsibilities between members of the project team unintentionally creates an apparent conflict of interest between those focusing on delivering fitness for purpose and those focusing on schedule and cost.

We have explained how this apparent conflict is an illusion; delivery of poor quality results in cost and delay, often many times greater than any 'savings' made by cutting corners on quality management. We have illustrated this with many examples, both of success and of disastrous failure. So long as anyone involved anywhere in the project is relaxed about letting a mistake or defect pass un-actioned, on the basis that someone else will pick it up later, or that they have followed the process, problems will grow rather than be solved. That means greater delays and more cost, eventually snatching defeat from the jaws of victory.

How can we heal the rift between those working to deliver quality (designers, architects, solution architects, systems engineers, quality experts etc) and those accountable for schedule and cost management (portfolio, programme and project managers, planners, accountants etc)?

It can only be through altering the perceptions that portfolio, programme and project managers have of quality, and helping them to understand why they would benefit from taking a greater focus on project quality management. The iron triangle is a useful tool to analyse the conflicting demands on a project, helping the

FIGURE 12.2 The Iron Pyramid – how quality underpins project success.

project team and stakeholders to reach agreement on the right balance between time, cost and quality objectives to maximise project success. Understanding how good quality management underpins project success leads to reshaping the iron triangle to give the 'iron pyramid'; quality supports timeliness through avoiding errors and rework; timeliness reduces delay costs (Figure 12.2).

Ultimately, project quality is the product of a culture in which delivering products on time that are fit for purpose and comply with requirements, is the norm. This is about **values, discipline and behaviour**; it can only be supported by processes and standards.

12.3 Bibliography

APM (2012) 'APM Body of Knowledge', 6th edition, Association for Project Management, ISBN: 9781903494400

Atkinson, R. (1999) 'Project management: cost, time and quality, two best guesses and a phenomenon, it's time to accept other success criteria.' International Journal of Project Management 17:6, 337–342.

GLOSSARY OF QUALITY TERMS

TABLE 12.2 Glossary of quality terms

Term	Definition
AQL	Acceptable quality level
Change request	Formal request to change the requirements or solution
Change Note	Approval for a requirement to be changed, with financial impacts accepted
Competence	Demonstrable ability to apply knowledge and skills
Concession	Permission to use or release a product that does not conform to specified requirements
Conformity or conformance	Fulfilment of a requirement
Contingency plan	Pre-planned set of Corrective Actions should an issue occur
Contract	Binding agreement
Corrective action	Action to eliminate the cause of a detected nonconformity or other undesirable situation
Cost of Implementing Quality (CoIQ)	The cost of effort and resources to plan and implement the quality activities of the project
Effectiveness	Extent to which planned activities are realised and planned results achieved
Efficiency	Relationship between the result achieved and the resources used
Customer Satisfaction	Customer's perception of the degree to which the customer's requirements have been fulfilled
Inspection	A qualitative review of the fitness for purpose of a product. Conformity evaluation by observation and judgement accompanied as appropriate by measurement, testing or gauging
Knowledge management (KM)	The processes and tools for collecting knowledge about the business, distilling insights from it and sharing the results
Mitigation plan	Set of mitigating actions
Nonconformity Or non-conformance	Non-fulfilment of a requirement

Glossary of quality terms **179**

Term	Definition
Organisational structure	Arrangement of responsibilities, authorities and relationships between people
Outage	A planned shutdown to allow essential work to be carried out
PONC	Price of non-conformance, a measure of quality in financial terms. The total financial impact of all consequences if quality goals are NOT met
PRA Codes	Plant Reliability and Availability Codes
Preventive action	Action to eliminate the cause of a potential non-conformity or other undesirable potential situation
Product	Result of a process. In this book, it can refer to services, manufactured items, documents, competent people etc.
Project	Unique process undertaking consisting of a set of coordinated and controlled activities with start and finish dates
	Undertaken to achieve an objective conforming to specific requirements including the constraints of time, cost and resources
Project Quality Plan/Project Quality Strategy	A document describing the key control points through the life cycle of the workflow, together with the associated inspection and test requirements and acceptance criteria required at each control point before progressing to the next stage
Punch list	A list of outstanding activities to be completed prior to final acceptance of the deliverables or hand-over
Qualitative risk analysis	A generic term for subjective methods of assessing risks that cannot be identified measured accurately
Quality	The fitness for purpose or the degree of conformance to requirements
Quality assurance (QA)	The process of evaluating project performance on a regular basis to provide confidence that the project will satisfy the relevant quality standards, including conducting appropriate reviews at key points during the workflow
Quality assurance plan	A plan that guarantees a quality approach and conformance to all customer requirements for all activities in a project
Quality audit	An official examination to determine whether practices conform to specified standards or a critical analysis of whether a deliverable meets quality criteria
Quality control (QC)	The process of monitoring specific project results to determine if they comply with relevant standards and identifying ways to eliminate causes of unsatisfactory performance
Quality criteria	The characteristics of a product that determine whether it meets its requirements

(Continued)

180 Glossary of quality terms

TABLE 12.2 Continued

Term	Definition
Quality guide	The quality guide describes quality and configuration management procedures and is aimed at people directly involved with quality reviews, configuration management and technical exceptions
Quality management system	The complete set of quality standards, procedures and responsibilities for a site or organisation
Quality manual	Document specifying the quality management system of an organisation
Quality planning	The process of determining how fitness for purpose will be achieved and assessed, which includes which quality standards are necessary and the processes to apply them
Quality Register	Central repository for all quality plans and records within the project
Quality review	A review of a product against an agreed set of quality criteria
Requirement	Need or expectation that is stated, generally implied or obligatory Alternatively: Expression in the content of a document conveying criteria to be fulfilled if compliance with the document is to be claimed and from which no deviation is permitted
Review	Activity undertaken to determine the suitability, adequacy and effectiveness of the product to achieve its objectives
Risk	An uncertain event or condition that, were it to occur, would have a positive or negative effect on a project objective
Risk Assessment	An assessment of what could go wrong, the vulnerabilities that could cause this to happen, the probability of this happening, this impact of it happening and a consequential overall measure of risk (to allow ranking and therefore prioritisation)
Risk Control Measures	Steps taken to alleviate the impact of risk
Right first time	The outcome of excellent quality management. The target for Total Quality Management
Scope	The scope of a project is the sum total of its products. It is as defined by the product breakdown structure for the plan and its associated Product Descriptions and acceptance criteria, its stakeholders and its interactions with external actors
Standard Operating Procedures (SOP)	Sets of standard work instructions, designed to support human workers carry out a standard task in a consistent and repeatable way, leading to outcomes within tolerance
Test	An objective assessment quantitative review of a product's fitness for purpose against the specifications and acceptance criteria

Glossary of quality terms   **181**

Term	Definition
Total Cost of Ownership (TCO)	The complete set of costs associated with the procurement, operation and disposal of an asset, of which the purchase price may be a small fraction
TPIA	A third party inspection authority, used to carry out quality assessments independently of the supplier or customer
Total Quality Management (TQM)	A corporate ethos of getting quality right to improve commercial performance
Traceability	Ability to trace the history, application or location of that which is under consideration
Validation	Confirmation, through the provision of objective evidence, that the requirements for a product fulfil the needs
Verification	Confirmation, through the provision of objective evidence, that specified requirements have been fulfilled
Zero defects	The standard toward which quality management strives

APPENDIX CASE STUDY: GETTING THE BALANCE RIGHT – RION-ANTIRION BRIDGE

This highly successful project is included as it demonstrates the effective application of a quality-focused mind-set across all the disciplines of project management and the benefits to the project that resulted.

The Rion-Antirion Bridge's 2,252 m long, single piece, four-pylon cable-stayed deck is the longest cable-stayed suspended deck in the world. Figure 13.1 shows the bridge.

It spans the Gulf of Corinth, linking Rion, near Patras on the Peloponnese, to Antirion on the Greek mainland. Work began in July 1998, and the main construction was completed in May 2004, well ahead of the planned completion date. The bridge was formally opened in August 2004, a week **before** the Summer Olympics in Athens, rather than three months after, as originally planned.

Engineering challenges encountered in construction included strong winds, deep water, no secure foundations, major seismic activity and the requirement for the bridge span to increase at a rate of 7mm or more per annum due to tectonic plate movement throughout its working lifetime.

The pylons which support the bridge have no foundations in the seabed; their large flat bases are free to move on a layer of gravel-covered seabed, stabilised by inclusions, rather than supported rigidly on load-bearing piles. This means that during an earthquake, the gravel bed absorbs the transverse vibration energy. The bridge deck has no load-bearing connection direct to the pylons; it is fully suspended by the cables. The only other linkages between deck and pylon are dampers triggered to control movement in the event of an earthquake. The bridge is equipped with a health monitoring system that has a comprehensive set of sensors, including accelerometers, strain gauges, load cells, temperature sensors and water-level sensors in the pylon bases. It provides constant surveillance of the structure.

Figures 13.2–13.5 illustrate its construction approach, shown by models in the visitor centre.

Appendix case study: getting the balance right – Rion-Antirion Bridge

FIGURE 13.1 Rion-Antirion Bridge (Photograph © Andrew Wright)

Why is this presented as an example of a project quality success?

- It won the International Association for Bridge and Structural Engineering's Outstanding Structure Award in 2006 – **fit for purpose**.
- It was completed four months early, earning a large bonus (distributed to the team) – **on time**.
- The bridge cost approximately € 630 million and was completed within budget tolerance – **on budget.**
- There were no fatalities during this project – safe.

184 Appendix case study: getting the balance right – Rion-Antirion Bridge

FIGURE 13.2 Seabed was prepared for pylon base (Photograph © Andrew Wright)

- It survived all subsequent earthquakes as designed – **fit for purpose**.

How was this achieved? Quality was a focus of the project team from the start.
- Requirements: time was spent on making sure that the requirements were made clear and well documented.
- Leadership: technical focus rather than financial, looking for solutions to problems leading to a successful solution, not blame attribution.
- Standards, disciplines and processes: imposed clearly from the start of the project.
- Organisation: designed right at the start, with quality roles and responsibilities clearly defined, including independent teams for design audit and design calculation checks.

FIGURE 13.3 The pylon bases were constructed in dry dock (Photograph © Andrew Wright)

FIGURE 13.4 The partially completed bases were floated out for further construction in a wet dock, freeing the dry dock for the next two. Each pylon base was then towed to the prepared location and sunk, after which construction of the pylon was completed (Photograph © Andrew Wright)

FIGURE 13.5 Once the pylon was completed, deck sections were cantilevered out, held up by the stay cables (Photograph © Andrew Wright)

- Design: Designed for quality from the start, with all drawings in the central engineering data management system (EDMS) under strict change control. Only two instances found of the wrong drawing version in use over the whole project.
- Change control: rigorously applied, with Change management responsiveness targets included in the project's key performance indicators with a 30-day maximum turnaround time for approval/rejection of a change request.
- Quality methods: Checklists and method statements were all best practice. Independent inspection authorities were used.
- Non-conformance management was centralised in the same EDMS as the drawings, ensured that all information was held together in the same system – baseline design, what the non-conformance was, and any revision to the design.
- Team building: Spirits kept high due to management effort and lots of celebrations. Sub-contractor problems were shared by the project team, who helped to overcome the problem rather than criticise.
- Continuity from construction to maintenance; many workers stayed on after completion to maintain the bridge.

- Safety: 30-minute safety workshops were held every two weeks with input sought from everyone. consequently, there were no fatalities on the project.
- 'Green' waste and energy management were designed into the project and executed as planned.
- Strong risk management:
  3) Computer forecasts indicated that the longest stay cables would need dampers to control wind-induced resonance. As the dampers would cost £3 million, and the need was unproven, a 'wait and see' approach was chosen, but in mitigation, the mounting points for the dampers were included, at low cost, during the build. Once in use, it became clear the forecast was correct and the dampers were needed – it was then simple to fit them (Figure 13.6 shows the dampers now in place).
  4) Expansion joints capable of withstanding any foreseeable earthquake were very expensive to buy and maintain. It was decided that replacements for simpler joints could be fitted after any strong earthquake and this was a more cost-effective solution.
- Pragmatic issue management: constructing the bridge involved sinking the pylons into place on the seabed. This was a complex process due to sea currents and boat movement, as well as the weight of the pylon, to take into consideration. After the first pylon was lowered into place, it was discovered that it

FIGURE 13.6 Dampers now in place (Photograph © Andrew Wright)

was 30 cm from its target location, well outside the tolerance of 10 cm. Rather than undertake the cost and risk of raising the pylon, moving and re-sinking it, the project team decided to adjust the design of the bridge to accommodate the new position of the first pylon.

This case study is a clear example of how putting quality first resulted in project success, while meeting schedule and budget constraints.

INDEX

acceptable quality level (AQL) 13, 178
acceptance 63, 65–9, 74, 97–9; acceptable standards 63; acceptance testing 20–21, 63, 65–9, 71, 74, 86, 87, 97, 98, 107, 124, 125, 144, 159; criteria for, need for clarity in 97–9; operational acceptance testing (OAT) 155; project lifecycle, quality management throughout 74; quality management, building acceptance of 39–42; tools for, quality outputs and 74
agile methodologies 125
American Society for Quality (ASQ) 25
American Society of Civil Engineers (ASCE) 72
approval records 63, 71–3
Association for Project Management (APM) 1; Body of Knowledge (BoK) 4, 11, 23, 53, 56, 122, 125–7, 129, 145; MoSCoW classification system 123–4; Project Quality Plan (2012) 57, 62, 127; Project Risk Assessment and Management method 129–30
assurance *see* quality assurance
Atkinson, R. 2, 172
Australian Transport Safety Bureau (ATSB) 24
automotive manufacturing 96
availability, reliability and maintainability (ARM) 123

Bacon, Francis 138
balance, getting it right 18–19m 182–8

Barnes, Martin 1, 171, 172–3
Barnes Triangle *see* Iron Triangle
behaviours, project quality and 32, 33, 40, 46, 49, 177; behavioural safety 155; group behaviours 44
benchmarking 167
benefits: business benefits, definition and quantification of 29; commercial benefits, delivery through quality 24–6; of effectiveness in quality management 18–26; project management maturity, benefits realization 167; realization stage 77–8; standard operating procedures (SOPs), benefits from 168–9
Bicheno, John 115
Bismarck, Otto 140
brainstorming 115
British Airports Authority (BAA) 100
British Airways (BA) 76
British Petroleum (BP) Texas City refinery 114
British Standards Institute (BSI) 4, 13, 51, 52, 55, 135, 162–5
budgets 1, 10, 12, 17–21, 63, 65, 67, 132, 160; authorisation of 26; balance of schedule with 121, 144; contingency time buffers and budgets 129, 131; cross-disciplinary control of 2; delivery on budget 22–3, 100; over-runs 43, 106, 125, 136; project budget 172–6; target costs and 167
build stage in project lifecycle 63, 71–3; tools, quality outputs and 71

190 Index

Bureau d'Enquêtes et d'Analyses pour la Sécurité de l'Aviation Civile (BEA) 151–2
business as usual 146, 153
business performance *see* performance
business process change, training and 153

capability 12, 27, 85, 86, 116, 132, 137, 158; manufacturing capability 95; technical capability 45
capability maturity models *see* maturity models
Cartlidge, D. 56, 66
case studies: Air France Airbus AF-447 A330 lost over South Atlantic 151–2; balance, getting it right 18–19; balance and getting it right 182–8; cascading quality down supply chain 95; Channel Tunnel, supply chain conflict on project 43; chemical plant project acceptance problems 98; Colombia space shuttle 20; core system replacement for credit card providers 118–19; critical success criteria driving project approach 9–10; financial services compliance project 137–8; getting incentives wrong 105; Heathrow Terminal 5, integration testing inadequacy 76; Hyatt Regency Hotel, walkway collapse in Kansas City 72; ICL Peripherals, team working in supply chain 35–6; inappropriate materials for safety-critical application, supply of 56; insurance, profitability in 142; interface design, failure of 151–2; large customers, close collaboration with 100; management information system 159; Millennium Dome, technical success, commercial failure 65; nuclear facility seismic certification 73; profitability in insurance 142; project approach, critical success criteria driving 9–10; quality incentives success 104; quality risk management, getting it right 128–9; quality risk management, getting it wrong 128; Rion-Antirion Bridge 18–19, 21, 182–8; risk contingency 133; risk mitigation 132–3; safety, Colombia space shuttle and 20; Scottish Parliament Building, changing requirements 66; small customers, minimal purchasing power and 100; speciality coatings 97; supplier replacement with quality supplier 95; Teton Dam, design unfit for purpose 70; Three Mile Island

nuclear incident 88–90; Trent engine manufacturing changes 24
cause and effect diagrams 110
CE mark 166
change control 19, 42, 54, 56, 57, 59, 63, 64–9, 71, 74, 75, 85, 97, 125–6; configuration management and 55, 143; definition of 125–6; of paperwork, difficulties in 149; process of 127; waterfall methodology and 145–6
change fatigue 36–7
change management discipline 126–7
change note 178
change request 178
Channel Tunnel, supply chain conflict on project 43
check sheets 110
checklists 169, 186
chemical plant project acceptance problems 98
coding, software ('V model' of system development) 146
Colombia space shuttle 20
commercial factors, quality and 45
commissioning 63, 75; costs of 29; quality delivery and 87; test of 53; tools for, quality outputs and 75
communication 44, 94, 139, 141, 168; channels of, tasking for quality 84; communication errors 56; contracting and 68; knowledge sharing and 138; management communication 113; remote forms of 83
competence 163, 165, 178
competition 137
compliance specialists 34
component build 53
component test 53
computer aided design (CAD) systems 141
concept stage, project lifecycle 63
concessions 14, 60, 77, 178
conformance 44, 99, 178; measurement of 87; non-conformance 58, 60, 77, 87, 99, 178; to requirements 3, 4, 5, 15, 20, 50, 122, 143, 168; *see also* price of non-conformance (PONC)
contingency plans 128, 129, 131, 132, 133, 178; risk and 167
continuous improvement 8–9, 11, 51, 53, 100, 101, 107, 110, 114–15, 116, 119, 163, 164
contract 23, 26, 43, 58, 60, 63, 68–9, 71, 74–5, 77–8, 97–8, 103, 105, 178; contract changes 21, 131; contract

management 146, 149; contract quality plans 41, 93

contracting 62, 63, 64, 68–9; sub-contracting 39; tools for, quality outputs and 68

control: control charts 110; quality control (QC) 7–8, 11, 24, 50, 58, 60, 63, 75, 147–8, 179; system requirements 155, 156–7

Cooke-Davis, Terry 168

corporate culture change, introductory steps 37

corporate management 34

corrective action 58, 60–61, 71, 74–5, 77, 95–6, 111, 113, 178

cost and time trade-offs, balancing of 11

cost of failure to conform 13–15; trade-off between cost of achievement and 14, 15; *see also* price of non-conformance (PONC)

cost of implementing quality (CoIQ) 14, 28, 52, 174, 178

cost of quality 14, 15, 29

cost total, quality target and 14, 15

Cousins, P., Lamming, R., Lawson, B. and Squire, B. 99, 101

credit card providers, core system replacement for 118–19

critical path 42, 175

critical success criteria 64, 124; project approach driver 9–10

Crosby, P.B. 4, 13

cultural factors 45

culture change 33, 37, 98

culture of quality, need for 176–7

customer expectations 5, 23, 97, 126, 167

customer experience 9–10

customer feedback 148

customer needs 6

customer requirements 20, 21, 117, 126, 173, 179

customer satisfaction 17, 18, 22, 23, 26, 30, 48, 94, 96, 163, 167, 172, 178

customers 4, 5, 25, 33–4, 36, 51, 53, 63, 95, 101, 103, 105, 123–6, 128, 133, 146, 161, 164, 173; large customers, close collaboration with 100; quality flows for 54; small customers, minimal purchasing power and 100

Dale, B.G., Bamford, D. and van der Iwaarden, J. 26

Dale, B.G. van der Wiele, T. and van der Iwaarden, J. 26, 33, 38, 49, 51

data collection, project quality 7, 116, 157

decommissioning stage, project lifecycle 63, 78

definition stage, project lifecycle 63–4

delegated inspection authorities 44–6

deliverables 1, 8, 13, 17, 30, 35, 53, 55, 59, 71, 104, 147, 179

delivery quality, standards and 169

delivery stage, project lifecycle 64–75

Deming, W. Edwards 7

Deming Cycle (PDCA) 110, 115–16

design 39, 41, 43, 62, 63, 64, 65, 173, 186; computer aided design (CAD) systems 141; delivery stage 69; design challenges 18; design change 72; design documentation 71, 73, 74, 75, 77, 85; design failure 78; design fault 59; design issues (technical queries) 85; design specification 71; design stage 50, 59; design tolerances 85–6, 103, 109–10; documentation 63; interface design, failure of 151–2; interface design, inclusion of user in system 150; project lifecycle, quality management throughout 69–70; for quality 19; solution design 66; specifications 53, 146; structured systems analysis and design method (SSADM) 145; system design 141, 150, 159; Teton Dam, design unfit for purpose 70; tools for, quality outcomes and 69; verification 53, 146

desk working, quality in 81

detection of defects 52, 74, 125; detection costs 52–3

discipline, project quality and 177

document management, enterprise content and 140–41

documented requirements 122

'drop-in' training sessions (for IT systems) 153

dynamic systems development method (DSDM) 145, 147–9; principles of 148

earned value method 107, 176

economic factors, quality and 45

effectiveness 7, 39, 52, 68, 82, 83, 116, 150, 161, 166, 178; effective change control system, features of 126; management effectiveness 119, 128; in quality management, benefits of 18–26; team effectiveness 139; time in meetings, effectiveness of 82; *vs.* efficiency 135

efficiency 19, 135, 136, 137, 150, 152, 154, 161–2, 164, 166, 169, 178

192 Index

e-mail working 83
engineering data management systems
   (EDMSs) 19, 141, 186
enterprise content and document
   management 140–41
Environmental Protection Agency
   (EPA) 168–9
European Commission directives 24, 166
external services 44–6
extranet sites 141

factory production environment 85–7
factory test environment 86–7
failure costs 14, 15, 52
Feigenbaum, Armand 7–8
financial quality achievement
   premiums 102
financial quality failure penalties 103
fitness for purpose requirements 3, 4,
   5, 15
Five Whys (5Ys) analysis technique 107,
   110, 111–13, 119
flowcharts 168
Franklin, Benjamin 22

Gallup organization 25
Geller, E. Scott 155
Genuine/true requirements 122
getting quality incentives wrong 105
Gil, Nuno 100
go-live stage 76–7
Golden Triangle *see* Iron Triangle
group working *vs.* team working 44, 46
Gucci, Aldo 22

hand-over stage 63, 76–7
hand-over tools, quality outputs and 77
health and safety specialists 34
Heathrow Terminal 5, integration testing
   inadequacy 76
Hellard, Ron B. 93
Hendricks, K.B. and Singhal, V.R. 25
histograms 110
Hutchens, S. 25
Hyatt Regency Hotel, walkway collapse
   in Kansas City 72

ICL Peripherals, team working in supply
   chain 35–6
Imai, Masaaki 114–15
impact assessment 126, 139, 172
Inc. Magazine 63
incremental (agile) methods 147–9;
   advantages of 149; disadvantages of 149

The Independent 43
information sources 106
innovation 44, 69, 137, 151, 164
insight, distillation of data into 141–2
inspection 45, 49–50, 59–60, 63, 178, 181;
   delegated inspection authorities 44–6;
   equipment 63; plan 63; third party
   inspection authorities (TPIAs) 45, 181
Institute of Civil Engineers (ICE) 18
integration 63; project lifecycle and 75;
   quality delivery into 87; test 53, 146;
   tools for, quality outputs and 75
interface design: failure of 151–2; inclusion
   of user in system 150
International Computers Limited (ICL)
   149–50
International Conference on Quality
   Control (Tokyo, 1969) 7–8
International Electrotechnical Commission
   (IEC) 155
International Maritime Organization
   (IMO) 74
investment cost 52
Iron Triangle: Atkinson's dispute about
   adequacy of 172; balance of quality,
   time and cost 2, 171–6, 177; Barnes'
   goal for 172; cost 177; cost is everything
   (zone 1) 173, 174; fixed deadline, quality
   must be met, sponsor prepared to pay
   (zone 5) 173; immovable deadline
   (zone 2) 173, 174–5; inflexibility of time
   and cost (zone 4) 173, 174–5; of project
   management 2; quality 177; quality must
   be delivered within budget, no time
   constraint (zone 6) 173; requirements
   must be met (zone 3) 173; timeliness
   177; zones for quality management
   impact 172–6
ISO 9000 4, 51, 135, 162–3
ISO 9001 161, 162, 163–4
ISO 9004 162, 164
ISO 10006 162, 165
ISO 10007 55
ISO 19011 162, 164–5
ISO standards 158, 161–5, 169
ISO/TR 1017 109
IT project quality management 144–60;
   business process change, training and
   153; control system requirements 155,
   156–7; 'drop-in' training sessions 153;
   dynamic systems development method
   (DSDM) 147–8, 149; principles of
   148; incremental (agile) methods
   147–9; advantages of 149; disadvantages

Index **193**

of 149; interface design, inclusion of user in system 150; IT testing, types of 158; performance and non-functional requirements, dealing with 154–5; phased development 149–50; progress comparison, agile and waterfall approaches 148; quality challenges in training full-time users 152–3; quality challenges in training part-time users 153; random testing 158–9; reading suggestions 160; requirements, goals and 145–50; safety-critical requirements 155, 156–7; scheduling training, availability of training system 153; testing and acceptance of IT solutions 155–9; training, scope of 153; training full-time users, quality challenges in 152–3; training in use of IT solutions, people and 152–3; training part-time users, quality challenges in 153; 'V Model' of system development 146; waterfall structured methods 145–7; advantages of 145–6; disadvantages of 146–7

Jobs, Steve 63
Juran, J.M. and Godfrey, B. 5
Juran, Joseph M. 7

Kaizen 110, 114–15
Karim, K. Marosszeky, M. and Davis, S. 93
key performance indicators (KPIs) 135, 136–7, 138; selection of 136
Kipling, Rudyard 2
Kitemark 165–6
knowledge and information, filing and publication of 140–41
knowledge capture, management and sharing 136–42
knowledge management (KM) 138, 139–40, 178
Krause, D.R., Scannell, T.V. and Calantone, R.J. 101

language factors, quality and 45
leaders' quality responsibilities 37–8
Lean Thinking, concept of 8
learning from experience 8, 9, 73, 164
legal compliance 45
lessons learned logs, quality plans and 140
location of quality management 80–91; commissioning, quality delivery into 87; communication channels, tasking for quality 84; desk working 81;

e-mail working 83; factory production environment 85–7; factory test environment 86–7; integration, quality delivery into 87; IT systems supporting quality management 81; maintenance, quality in 90; meeting rooms 81–2; office environment 80–84; operation, quality in 87–8; paperwork 82–3; production of quality products 85–7; quality, communication channels and tasking for 84; remote forms of communication, working with 83–4; site environment 87–8; telephone working 83

maintenance 63, 77–8; quality in 90
major projects, requirements for 66–7
management information system 159
Manchester University 172
maturity models 137, 162, 167
McCallum, I. 12
McLoughlin, Paul 25
meaning of quality 3–4
measurement of quality 12–15
meetings, managing quality in 81–2
middle managers' quality responsibilities 38
Millennium Dome, technical success, commercial failure 65
minimal cost, quality target for 14, 15
mitigation: mitigation plans 132, 133, 178; risk mitigation 130, 132–3
monitoring quality 20, 38, 60, 132, 136, 155–6, 164, 168, 169, 182

National Aeronautics and Space Administration (NASA) 20, 22, 93–4, 138
National Audit Office (NAO) 65
New York Times 74
Nicholson, John 43, 167
non-conformances 58, 60, 77, 87, 99, 178; *see also* price of non-conformance (PONC)
non-conformance price 29
non-functional requirements 123

Oakland, J.S. and Marosszeky, M. 8
office environment, managing quality in the 80–84
operations: project lifecycle and 77–8; quality in 87–8
operative acceptance testing (OAT) 155
organisational responsibilities 36–9
organisational structure 179

194 Index

outages 90, 154, 179
Oxford English Dictionary 96

paperwork, role in quality 82–3
partnership strength, principles for
development of 104–6
performance: improvement of, project
management maturity and 166–8;
management and measurement of
135–7; and non-functional requirements,
dealing with 154–5
phased development, value in improving
quality 149–50
Plan-Do-Check-Act Cycle (PDCA) 110,
115–16
planning 63; for acceptance from start 124;
project lifecycle, quality management
throughout 67; project management 9;
for risks 129; tools for, quality outputs
and 67
portfolio/programme/project office
(PMO) 142
prevention costs 52; appraisal costs and 14, 15
price of non-conformance (PONC) 13–15,
28, 29, 101, 179
PRINCE2® 4, 11, 15n1, 17, 39–40, 54,
59, 129; quality management, project
lifecycle and 62, 64, 71
priority-balancing 1, 2, 3
procurement processes, synergies between
supplier quality assurance and 94
procurement specialists 34
production of quality products 85–7
product xv, 3, 4, 5, 8, 54, 179
products 179; initial purchase price of
29; product acceptance 63; product
acceptance criteria 63; product
acceptance test plans 63; product
descriptions 63; product quality criteria
63; product quality responsibilities 63;
product quality standards 165–6; product
requirements 63
programme management 34
progress comparison, agile and waterfall
approaches 148
project acceptance 63
project acceptance criteria 63
project acceptance test plans 63
project board 34
project definition 63
project lifecycle 49
project lifecycle, quality management
throughout 62–79; acceptance 74;
acceptance tools, quality outputs

and 74; approval records 71–3; benefits
realization stage 77–8; build stage 71–3;
build stage tools, quality outputs and 71;
commissioning 75; commissioning tools,
quality outputs and 75; concept stage
63; contracting 68–9; contracting tools,
quality outputs and 68; decommissioning
stage 78; definition stage 63–4; delivery
stage 64–75; design 69–70; design tools,
quality outcomes and 69; go-live stage
76–7; hand-over stage 76–7; hand-over
tools, quality outputs and 77; integration
75; integration tools, quality outputs and
75; maintenance 77–8; major projects,
requirements for 66–7; operations 77–8;
planning 67; planning tools, quality
outputs and 67; project definition
tools, quality outcomes and 64; quality
records 71–3; quality tools and lifecycle
stages, relationship between 63; reading
suggestions 79; requirements capture
65–6; requirements capture tools,
quality outputs and 65; stages in project
lifecycles 62–3; take-over stage 76–7;
take-over tools, quality outputs and 77;
warranty period 78
project management 34; conformance to
requirements 3, 4, 5, 15; cost and time
trade-offs, balancing of 11; elements of
2–3; fitness for purpose requirements 3,
4, 5, 15; Iron Triangle of 2; maturity,
indicators of 167; maturity, performance
improvement and 166–8; planning 9;
priority-balancing challenges in 1, 2, 3
Project Management Institute (PMI) 1, 62
project management techniques 121–43;
agile methods 125; change control
125–7; change control, definition
of 125–6; change control process
127; change management discipline
126–7; contingency time buffers and
budgets 131; critical success criteria
124; definition of requirements 124;
document management, enterprise
content and 140–41; documented
requirements 122; effective change
control system, features of 126;
effectiveness *vs.* efficiency 135;
engineering data management
systems (EDMSs) 141; enterprise
content, document management
and 140–41; extranet sites 141;
functional requirements 123; genuine
requirements 122; insight, distillation

of data into 141–2; key performance indicators (KPIs), selection of 136; knowledge and information, filing and publication of 140–41; knowledge capture, management and sharing 136–42; knowledge management (KM) 138–9; knowledge management (KM) tools 139–40; lessons learned logs, quality plans and 140; non-functional requirements 123; performance management and measurement 135–7; planning for acceptance from start 124; planning for risks 129; project acceptance, requirements verification and 125; project lifecycle choice 124–5; project performance, measurement of 135–7; project performance measurement, quality delivery and 135–7; projects, inter-related elements in 126; quality delivery, project performance in 135–7; quality plans, lessons learned logs and 140; reading suggestions 143; requirement prioritisation 123–4; requirements 122; requirements capture 124; requirements management 122–5; requirements validation 124–5; requirements verification, project acceptance and 125; responses to risk 131; risk assessment 130–31; risk avoidance 131; risk control during projects 132; risk identification 129–30; risk log template 134; risk management, application of 127–34; risk management, setting up for 129–32; risk management aims 128; risk management in project quality 127–34; risk management tools 133–4; risk mitigation 130; risk priority 131; risk response management 131–2; risk retention 131; risk sharing 131; risk transfer 131; risk urgency 131; specification 123; true requirements 122; usability, role of user in ensuring 124; waterfall methods 125
project quality 179; management of, roles and responsibilities in 40; plans 54, 56–7, 61, 65, 67–9, 71, 74–5, 77, 179; strategy 179; *see also* published standards, role in project quality
project quality flows 54
project quality management (PQM) 3
project quality management (PQM) strategy 63
project quality requirements 63

project success, balancing Iron Triangle and 171–7; behaviour, project quality and 177; culture of quality, need for 176–7; discipline, project quality and 177; Iron Triangle: Atkinson's dispute about adequacy of 172; balance of quality, time and cost 2, 171–6, 177; Barnes' goal for 172; cost is everything (zone project success, balancing Iron Triangle and 171–7; behaviour, project quality and 177; culture of quality, need for 176–7; discipline, project quality and 177; Iron Triangle: Atkinson's dispute about adequacy of 172; balance of quality, time and cost 2, 171–6, 177; Barnes' goal for 172; cost is everything (zone 1) 173, 174; fixed deadline, quality must be met, sponsor prepared to pay (zone 5) 173; immovable deadline (zone 1) 173, 174; fixed deadline, quality must be met, sponsor prepared to pay (zone 5) 173; immovable deadline (zone 2) 173, 174–5; inflexibility of time and cost (zone 4) 173, 174–5; quality must be delivered within budget, no time constraint (zone 6) 173; requirements must be met (zone 3) 173; zones for quality management impact 172–6; values, project quality and 177
project team costs 29
project teams 34
projects 179; budget 131, 172; construction projects 93, 133; definition tools, quality outcomes and 64; inter-related elements in 126; lifecycle choice 124–5; project acceptance, requirements verification and 125; project approach, critical success criteria driving 9–10; project assurance 46; project team, quality and 43–4
published standards, role in project quality 161–70; CE mark 166; delivery quality, standards and 169; ISO 9000 162–3; ISO 9001 161, 162, 163–4; ISO 9004 162, 164; ISO 10006 162, 165; ISO 19011 162, 164–5; ISO standards 161–5, 169; Kitemark 165–6; performance improvement, project management maturity and 166–8; product quality standards 165–6; project management maturity, benefits realisation 167; project management maturity, indicators of 167; project management maturity, performance improvement and 166–8;

196 Index

published standards (*Continued*)
quality management, standards supporting 162–6; standard operating procedures (SOPs), benefits from 168–9; standard operating procedures (SOPs), effective use of, challenges for 168–9

qualitative assessment of quality 13
qualitative risk analysis 179
quality 179; agreed vocabulary on 3; cascading quality down supply chain 95; communication channels and tasking for 84; cost of failure to conform 13–15; cost of failure to conform, trade-off between cost of achievement and 14, 15; definitions of 4–5; 'grade' 5; International Conference on Quality Control (Tokyo, 1969) 7–8; interpretations of term 3; Lean Thinking, concept of 8; meaning of 3–4; measurement of 12–15; as 'meeting requirements' 5–7; 'over-specification' 5, 42, 66; price of non-conformance (PONC) 13–15; project team and 43–4; qualitative assessment of quality 12; quality achievement premiums 102–3; quality management: continuous improvement 11; defect detection 11; defect prevention 11; economic lifetime 11; history of 7–9; in project context 11–12; in projects and manufacturing, differences between 8–9; quality assurance 11; quality control 11; quality planning 11; total cost of ownership (TCO) 11; quality management, growth of practice of 7–8; qualitative assessment of quality 13; right first time, principle of 7, 12, 13; shared understanding of 3; Six Sigma, concept of 8; statistical analysis of quality data 7; target setting for 12; right first time target 13; zero defects target 13; zero defects, principle of 7, 13; *see also* responsibility for quality
quality analysis techniques 107–20; accuracy and precision, difference between 108; accuracy in measurement and analysis 108–9; cause and effect diagrams 110; check sheets 110; continuous improvement (Kaizen) 114–15; control charts 110; defects waste 117, 118; Deming Cycle (PDCA) of continuous improvement 115–16; Five Whys (5Ys) analysis technique 111–13; flow charts 110; histograms 110; inventory

waste 117; measurement and analysis 108–9; mitigating actions in quality achievement 113–14; motion waste 117; normal distribution 109; over-processing waste 117, 118; over-production waste 117, 118; Pareto analysis 110–11; pattern recognition 114; physical separation 114; precision in measurement and analysis 108–9; prevention actions in quality achievement 113–14; process mapping 118; quality management techniques 110; reading suggestions 119–20; root cause analysis 111–13; scatter diagrams 110; Seven Lean Wastes 116–18; Seven Quality Tools 110–11; simple physical devices 114; standard deviation 109; tally charts 110; transport waste 117; visual signals 114; waiting waste 117; wastes, identification of 116–18
quality assurance (QA) 42, 49, 50–51, 60–61; quality assurance plan 179
quality audit 168, 179
quality control (QC) 49, 54, 63, 179
quality costs 14, 15, 29
quality criteria 41, 42, 56, 63, 64–77, 179
quality culture 33–5
quality delivery, project performance for 135–7
quality failure penalties 103
quality focus 49
quality guide 180
quality incentives 102–4
quality investment increase 29
quality management 17–32; acceptance criteria 56; acceptance report 60; benefits of effectiveness in 18–26; building acceptance of 39–42; business justification for rebalance of focus on quality, creation of 26–30; business outcomes 55; commercial benefits, delivery through quality 24–6; conformance to requirements 20, 30; contracts, delivery of quality through 58; corrective action request 60; cost control improvement through 20–21; cost-cutting, project risks from 27; cost of implementing quality (CoIQ) 14, 28, 52, 174, 178; cost reduction through investment in quality early in project lifecycle 52–3; customer satisfaction through 22–4; customer-supplier relationships 23; delay avoidance through 21–2; fire-fighting, need to see past 26–7; fitness for purpose

requirements 17, 20, 24, 30; growth of practice of 7–8; inspection 49–50; investment in quality early in project lifecycle, cost reduction through 52–3; need for 48–61; price of non-conformance (PONC) 28, 29; project change control and configuration (version) management 55; project delay reduction, trade-off between quality planning and 22; project execution, tools for delivery of quality during 58–60, 61; project initiation, toolkit for delivery success during 53–8, 61; project lifecycle, cost reduction through investment in quality early in 52–3; project morale, improvements in 26; project quality, construction of case for 28–30; approval process, understanding of 28; business benefits, definition and quantification of 29; business case presentation, creation of 30; champion, identification of 28; hard data justification of business case 29–30; stakeholder support, winning of 29; project quality plan 56–7; purpose to be fulfilled 55; quality: continuous improvement 11; defect detection 11; defect prevention 11; economic lifetime 11; history of 7–9; in project context 11–12; in projects and manufacturing, differences between 8–9; quality assurance 11; quality control 11; quality planning 11; total cost of ownership (TCO) 11; quality, commercial benefits of delivery through 24–6; quality and liability 23–4; quality assurance 50–51; quality control 50; quality criteria 56; quality failures, detection of 50; quality flow diagram 54; quality improvement, schematic financial breakdown for 29; quality in cost escalation avoidance 21; quality in rework avoidance 20–21; quality management system (QMS) 40, 49, 51–2, 57, 73, 82–3, 163–4; quality methods 56; quality methods, test and inspection techniques 59; quality planning 23, 50; quality register 58–9; quality thinking, advancing scope of 49; reading suggestions 31, 61; requirements and acceptance criteria 55–6; roles and responsibilities in 40; safety improvement through 19–20; scope of quality management 48–9, 78; evolving nature of 49; standards 56; standards

supporting 162–6; supplier's quality plan 57; test/inspection equipment 59; test/inspection log 59–60; test/inspection plan 59; timeliness improvement through 21–2; tolerances 56; total quality management (TQM) 8, 11, 48, 49, 51, 60–61, 96, 181; total quality management (TQM), winners using 25–6; unfashionable nature of 1–2; 'V Model,' schematics of project lifecycle 53; validation 53; verification 53; waste, cutting out of 27–8, 31; *see also* IT project quality management; location of quality management; project lifecycle, quality management throughout; supply chain quality management

quality management system (QMS) 40, 49, 51–2, 57, 73, 82–3, 163–4, 180

quality manual 180

quality methods 63

quality-oriented work in teams 33

quality planning 54, 63, 180; lessons learned logs and 140

quality progress, investment cost and 52

quality records 63, 71–3

Quality Register 63, 180

quality-related roles within projects 39–44

quality review 180

quality risk management: getting it right 128–9; getting it wrong 128

quality target 14, 15

quality tools and lifecycle stages, relationship between 63

radio frequency identification devices (RFIDs) 85, 95

random testing 158–9

rapid application development (RAD) 147, 148–9

reading suggestions: IT project quality management 160; project lifecycle, quality management throughout 79; project management techniques 143

regulatory compliance 45

relational quality achievement premiums 102

relational quality failure penalties 103

relationships with suppliers, quality and 101

remote forms of communication, working with 83–4

repeatability 8, 108, 181

reproducibility 108, 166

198 Index

reputational quality achievement premiums 103

reputational quality failure penalties 103

requirements 54, 63, 180; documentation, need for clarity in 96–7; goals and 145–50; prioritisation of 123–4; project management techniques 122; requirements capture 65–6, 124; requirements capture tools, quality outputs and 65; specifications and, distinction between 123

requirements management 122–5

requirements validation 53, 124–5, 146

requirements verification, project acceptance and 125

responsibility for quality: building acceptance of quality management 39–42; commercial factors 45; corporate culture change, introductory steps 37; cultural factors 45; delegated inspection authorities 44–6; economic factors 45; everyone's responsible 32–3; external services 44–6; group working *vs.* team working 44, 46; language factors 45; large projects, quality-related roles and responsibilities in 41; leaders' quality responsibilities 37–8; legal compliance 45; middle managers' quality responsibilities 38; organisational responsibilities 36–9; project assurance 46; project quality management, roles and responsibilities in 40; project team, quality and 43–4; quality and project team 43–4; quality culture 33–5; quality management, building acceptance of 39–42; quality management, roles and responsibilities in 40; quality-oriented work in teams 33; quality-related roles within projects 39–44; regulatory compliance 45; roles and responsibilities in project quality management 40; scope of project team-working 34; senior managers' quality responsibilities 37–8; specifications and standards, value of 46; staff quality responsibilities 38–9; supervisors' quality responsibilities 38–9; suppliers' quality responsibilities 38–9; supply chain, quality responsibilities and 39; supply chains, additional quality roles and responsibilities in 42; team managers' quality responsibilities 38; team working vs. group working 44, 46; technical capability 45

return on investment (ROI) 167

reviews 3, 38, 57, 70, 82, 115, 164, 180; design review process 85; peer reviews 124; qualitative reviews 178; review tools 54, 55, 57; stage gate reviews 73; systematic reviews 96

Richards, K. 148

right first time, principle of 7, 12, 13, 180

Rion-Antirion Bridge 18–19, 21, 182–8

risk, quality 180; planning for 129; premiums and penalties, risks in use of 103–4; Project Risk Assessment and Management method 129–30; responses to 131; risk assessment 130–31, 180; risk avoidance 131; Risks, Assumptions, Issues and Dependencies (RAID) 130–31, 132

risk contingency 133

risk control measures 132, 180

risk identification 129–30

risk log template 134

risk management: aims of 128; application of 127–34; in project quality 127–34; setting up for 129–32; tools of 133–4

risk mitigation: case studies 132–3; project management techniques 130

risk priority 131

risk response management 131–2

risk retention 131

risk sharing 131

risk transfer 131

risk urgency 131

Rogers Commission (1986) 93, 94

roles and responsibilities in project quality management 40

root cause analysis 107, 110, 111, 119

Rose, K. 5

Røsjø, B. & Hauge, K. 74

Royce, Henry 22

Ryan, J. 25

safety 13, 17–19, 24, 30, 41, 45, 56, 73, 94; Colombia space shuttle and 20; safety-critical requirements in IT projects 144, 155, 156–7

sample size 12, 49

sample testing 158

Sargeant, A., Hudson, J. and Wilson, S. 24–5

scatter diagrams 110

scheduling training, availability of training system 153

Schewart control charts 7

scope of project team-working 34

scope of projects 12, 23, 34, 41, 50, 172, 180; scope creep 64

Index **199**

scope of quality management 48–9, 78
scope of training 153
Scottish Parliament Building, changing
   requirements 66
self-assessment 38, 164
senior managers' quality responsibilities 37–8
service level agreements (SLAs) 99, 128–9;
   in accepting services 99; example 99
Seven Lean Wastes 116–18
Seven quality tools 110–11
Shaw, George Bernard 45
site environment 87–8
Six Sigma, concept of 8
solution specifications 53, 146
Space Shuttle Challenger disaster: pre-
   launch conditions, delay and 93–4;
   Rogers Commission investigation 94;
   supply chain quality failures in 93–4
speciality coatings 97
specifications 15, 20, 50, 52–3, 56, 69, 71,
   74–5, 77, 98 117, 123, 143, 181; out of
   specification 99, 101; 'over-specification'
   5, 42, 66; requirements and, distinction
   between 123; standards and, value of 46;
   tolerances and 63, 68, 86
staff quality responsibilities 38–9
stage payments 43, 48, 60, 73, 159
stages in project lifecycles 62–3
standard operating procedures (SOPs) 90,
   140, 161, 168–9, 180; benefits from
   168–9; effective use of, challenges for
   168–9
standards, acceptability of 63
statistical process control (SPC) 7
structured systems analysis and design
   method (SSADM) 145
supervisors' quality responsibilities 38–9
supplier auditing, use in quality assurance
   of 96
supplier development, quality management
   and 101–2
supplier quality assurance and procurement
   processes, synergies between 94
suppliers 34, 53, 146; development of
   102; numbers of 102; progress on
   development 102; quality flows for 54;
   quality of 102; quality plans 63
supply chain quality management 92–106;
   acceptance criteria, need for clarity
   in 97–9; additional quality roles and
   responsibilities in supply chains 42;
   automotive manufacturing 96; financial
   quality achievement premiums 102;
   financial quality failure penalties 103;

information sources 106; partnership
   strength, principles for development
   of 104–6; procurement processes,
   synergies between supplier quality
   assurance and 94; quality achievement
   premiums 102–3; quality failure
   penalties 103; quality incentives 102–4;
   quality responsibilities 39; relational
   quality achievement premiums 102;
   relational quality failure penalties 103;
   relationships with suppliers, quality and
   101; reputational quality achievement
   premiums 103; reputational quality
   failure penalties 103; requirements
   documentation, need for clarity in 96–7;
   risks of using premiums and penalties
   103–4; service level agreement example
   99; service level agreements in accepting
   services 99; Space Shuttle Challenger
   disaster, supply chain quality malfunction
   in 93–4; strengths of using premiums
   and penalties 103; supplier auditing,
   use in quality assurance 96; supplier
   development, quality management
   and 101–2; supplier quality assurance
   and procurement processes, synergies
   between 94; supplier replacement with
   quality supplier 95; suppliers' quality
   responsibilities 38–9; supply chain
   quality, introduction to 92–4; supply
   chain quality malfunction 93–4
system design 141, 150, 159
systems thinking 33, 122, 124

take-over stage, project lifecycle 63, 76–7
take-over tools, quality outputs and 77
tally charts 110
target setting 12; 'right first time' target 13;
   zero defects target 13
Taylor, W.A. and Wright, G.H. 37
team managers' quality responsibilities 38
team working vs. group working 44, 46
technical queries 42, 85
telephone working 83
testing 2, 12, 22, 39, 45, 54–5, 57–60, 63,
   115, 119, 122, 131, 180; acceptance
   of IT solutions and 155–9; acceptance
   testing 20–21, 63, 65–9, 71, 74, 86, 87,
   97, 98, 107, 124, 125, 144, 159; factory
   test environment 86–7; Heathrow
   Terminal 5, integration testing
   inadequacy 76; operational acceptance
   testing (OAT) 155; quality methods,
   test and inspection techniques 59;

200 Index

testing (*Continued*)
    random testing 158–9; test equipment 63; test/inspection 59–60; test plan 63
Teton Dam, design unfit for purpose 70
third party inspection authorities (TPIAs) 45, 181
Three Mile Island nuclear incident 88–90
through-life costs 29
time in meetings, effectiveness of 82
tolerances 13, 18–19, 24, 42, 46, 54, 56, 63–5, 68–9, 71, 73–5, 77, 167, 181, 183, 188; design tolerances 85–6, 103, 109–10
total cost of ownership (TCO) 11, 30, 181
total quality management (TQM) 8, 11, 48, 49, 51, 60–61, 96, 181; winners using 25–6
traceability 154, 181
training: full-time users, quality challenges and 152–3; part-time users, quality challenges and 153; scope of 153; in use of IT solutions, people and 152–3
Transmanche Link (TML) 21, 43
Trent engine failure 24
true requirements 53, 122, 124, 147

unit test 146
Universal Modeling Language (UML) 158
usability, role of user in ensuring 124
user acceptance test 146
user requirements 53, 146

'V Model' of system development 53, 146
validation 53–4, 124, 125, 146, 149, 181
values 33, 37; project quality and 177; value stream mapping 118
verification 53–4, 69, 70, 125, 146, 149, 159, 181
version control 63

warranty 63
warranty period 78
waterfall methodologies 125, 145–7; advantages of 145–6; disadvantages of 146–7
Womack, J.P. and Jones, D.T. 96

Young, Ralph R. 22

Zero Defects, principle of 7, 13, 181